NEDLEY

Depression & Anxiety

Recovery

Program™

JOURNAL

NEIL NEDLEY, MD

Nedley Publishing
info@nedleyhealth.com
www.nedleyhealth.com

580.226.8007
888.778.4445

ISBN 13: 978-1-938028-14-4

Caution: This book and video series does not establish a doctor-patient relationship with the reader. Persons who are ill or on medication who wish to significantly change their lifestyle should do so under the direction of a physician familiar with the effects of lifestyle change on health.

Disclaimer: Dr. Nedley does not endorse all the views, opinions, or philosophies which may be advanced by the authors referenced in this book.

Special Thanks
Contributors: Jacob Metzner, Erica Nedley, and Kelli Daugherty
Editor: Kelli Daugherty
References: Cami Gotshall and Nathan Hyde
Layout and Design: Trap–Studio

Printed in China.

Welcome to the *Nedley Depression and Anxiety Recovery Program*™ Journal

The *Journal* is an interactive component of the program created for you to practice gratitude and to provide you opportunities to reflect on the importance and spiritual foundation of the new lifestyle habits you are learning. As you will see, each of the principles of health discussed in this program have a Scriptural basis; today's scientific research is in agreement with timeless Biblical concepts documented 2,000 to 3,000 years ago. Additionally, the Bible speaks of countless individuals who have gone before you in the battle against depression and anxiety. You will be inspired by the stories of people like you and encouraged by God's response to those who are hurting.

God taught us these principles to give us health. He desires for us to have a rich, abundant life. We hope that through this *Journal* you can be made aware of how much God loves you and how He has provided a means for you to obtain recovery. For some, spirituality may be a long-standing component of everyday life. For others, this may be a completely new experience. Whatever your path, come to each day with an open mind willing to learn, try new lifestyle and thought patterns, and experience God's healing power and love. As you engage in this *Journal*, expect to gain strength in self-control, which will enable you to make and stay with positive lifestyle and thought choices throughout your life.

Be fully open and honest with yourself and God. Think critically about your thoughts and reflect on what you are reading. Find joy in gratitude. Process what you need. Some of the prompts may be challenging and require time to work through. Take the time you need and come back to topics as you wish.

We recommend you set time aside each morning, about 30 minutes, for the next eight weeks to make this *Journal* part of your daily routine to reap the best results. The topics of this *Journal* follow the sessions from the *Nedley Depression and Anxiety Recovery Program*™ lectures and are meant to be read in conjunction with them. There are extra resources for reflective reading and practical sessions which we encourage you to do in addition to the main devotionals, but they can be done at a later time. Throughout this *Journal*, we also encourage you to read *Telling Yourself the Truth* by William Backus and Marie Chapian. These materials will provide you additional encouragement and insight into the topics presented.

We believe devotional time will become instrumental in your life. Following this *Journal*, we encourage you to continue with daily devotional studies. We recommend you study Psalms, Proverbs, or Daniel. Whatever you do, keep the principles you learn here in mind to further your learning and enrich your experience.

The *Nedley Depression and Anxiety Recovery Program*™ and its *Journal* are not a substitute for a physician, psychiatrist, or a counselor. If you are in need of help from such sources, you should not hesitate to seek it.

Nedley Health offers a residential *Nedley Depression and Anxiety Recovery Program*™. For more information go to: www.nedleyhealth.com/recovery. This program is a full therapeutic program plus a certified educational program, utilizing physicians, licensed counselors, therapists, registered nurses, and other trained personnel.

For community program locations and to learn more, visit: www.nedleyhealth.com/community-program/ programs-near-you

"Let all that I am praise the Lord;

with my whole heart, I will praise his holy name.

Let all that I am praise the Lord;

may I never forget the good things he does for me.

He forgives all my sins

and heals all my diseases.

He redeems me from death

and crowns me with love and tender mercies.

He fills my life with good things.

My youth is renewed like the eagle's!

The Lord gives righteousness

and justice to all who are treated unfairly.

He revealed his character to Moses

and his deeds to the people of Israel.

The Lord is compassionate and merciful,

slow to get angry and filled with unfailing love."

Psalm 103:1–8 (NLT)

Table of Contents

With God, Recovery Is Possible

WEEK 1

GRATITUDE

"THE QUALITY OF BEING THANKFUL; READINESS TO SHOW APPRECIATION FOR AND TO RETURN KINDNESS."[1]

Oxford English Dictionary

"THINK OF ALL THE WONDERFUL THINGS HE [THE LORD] HAS DONE FOR YOU."

1 Samuel 12:24 (NLT)

The Depressed Prophet

1 KINGS 19:4 (NLT)

"'I [Elijah] have had enough, Lord,' he said. 'Take my life, for I am no better than my ancestors who have died.'"

The Bible provides us numerous stories to teach us about life and God, bringing us comfort, peace, and hope. One such story is of a prophet of God who saw many miracles. But he, like us, struggled with depression and anxiety. His name was Elijah.

God's people, Israel, had generations of evil rulers who led them to worship other gods. The current king and queen, Ahaz and Jezebel, were no exception. Elijah the prophet was called by God to demonstrate to the people His character and lead them back to Him. In an incredible display to the nation, Elijah prayed to God and called fire down from heaven, through which the Lord revealed Himself as the true God to His people. The false prophets were killed, and the Israelites restored worship to God. Jezebel was furious. She had appointed the false prophets who were killed. In revenge, she threatened to kill Elijah. Elijah fled into the wilderness alone in fear. Hiding under a tree that night, he prayed to God that he might die. An angel appeared to him twice, bringing him food and water and encouraging the weary prophet to rest.

Elijah demonstrated many symptoms of depression and anxiety, including isolating himself, exhaustion, desiring to die, and distorted thinking. In his struggles and fears, he forgot the miraculous ways God had revealed Himself to him and how God had protected and preserved his life in the past. He hadn't asked God what to do. How did the Lord respond to Elijah? He sent an angel to take care of his needs. He gave Elijah food, water, rest, and protection in the wilderness. God did not answer Elijah's prayer that he would die, but instead never let Elijah see death—Elijah eventually was taken straight to heaven on a fiery chariot. God proclaimed Elijah righteous, even though he struggled with depression and anxiety (James 5:16–18).

God does not condemn us for our mental struggles. He cares deeply for each of us and gently treats those who are hurting. He will provide for all our needs.

As you embark on the journey of overcoming depression and anxiety, pray, asking God to strengthen and encourage you along the way. Here's an example of how you could pray: "God, You took care of Elijah, and I ask that You take care of me. In beginning this journey to overcome depression and anxiety, help me as I seek to know a better way."

Reflective Reading: 1 Kings 18–19:8

DAILY GRATITUDE

1 . . . .

. . . .

2 . . . .

. . . .

3 . . . .

. . . .

4 . . . .

. . . .

5 . . . .

. . . .

MY REFLECTION

. . . .

. . . .

. . . .

. . . .

. . . .

. . . .

. . . .

. . . .

. . . .

. . . .

. . . .

Depression and Anxiety: A Winnable War

2 TIMOTHY 1:7 (NLT)

"For God has not given us a spirit of fear and timidity, but of power, love, and self-discipline."

___

After Elijah's encounters with the angel, he traveled 40 days and nights to Mount Sinai, the Mountain of God. After spending the night in a cave, God spoke to Elijah, asking, "What are you doing here, Elijah?" (1 Kings 19:9, NLT). Elijah told God that he was the only one alive who faithfully served Him, and he was afraid because Jezebel wanted to kill him. God instructed Elijah to go outside and to stand before Him on the mountain. A strong wind appeared, breaking rocks into pieces. An earthquake followed, then a fire. But God wasn't in any of these. At the end of the raucous, Elijah heard a still, small voice, and he knew God was there. God asked His question a second time, "What are you doing here, Elijah?" (1 Kings 19:13, NLT). Elijah repeated his same answer. God gave a gentle response: He gave Elijah a calling, then reassured him that he was not alone—there were another 7,000 faithful in Israel who had never worshiped false gods.

Elijah had gotten lost in his cognitive distortions and negative thoughts. God met him where he was. He asked Elijah a question to help him evaluate his thoughts and actions. God revealed His presence, demonstrating that He is not in the boisterous calamities, but in the quiet moments as One who is gentle. After all this, God reaffirmed Elijah's calling as a prophet. God combated Elijah's distortion by speaking truth to him: not only was Elijah not alone because he wasn't the only one faithful, but he wasn't alone because God had always been with him.

As He did for Elijah, God will help you evaluate your thoughts. He will reveal His presence in your life, affirm the calling He has given to you, and combat your distorted thinking with the truth. You are never alone because God is with you, and He is actively working on your behalf. You are not the only one struggling—others are also battling depression and anxiety. There are others, like Elijah, who have successfully completed this journey, and with God's help you can complete it, too. The war against depression and anxiety is winnable.

Pray, asking God to help you evaluate your thoughts and understand the truth. Here is an example: "God, only You know the intricacies and innermost struggles of my mind. Help me evaluate my thoughts. Teach me to know and believe the truth. Win this war and set me free."

Reflective Reading: John 17:17

DAILY GRATITUDE

1 . . . .
. . . .

2 . . . .
. . . .

3 . . . .
. . . .

4 . . . .
. . . .

5 . . . .
. . . .

MY REFLECTION

. . . .
. . . .
. . . .
. . . .
. . . .
. . . .
. . . .
. . . .
. . . .
. . . .
. . . .

A Grateful Heart

PSALM 100 (NLT)

"Shout with joy to the Lord, all the earth! Worship the Lord with gladness. Come before him, singing with joy. Acknowledge that the Lord is God! He made us, and we are his. We are his people, the sheep of his pasture. Enter his gates with thanksgiving; go into his courts with praise. Give thanks to him and praise his name. For the Lord is good. His unfailing love continues forever, and his faithfulness continues to each generation."

PROVERBS 17:22 (NIV)

"A cheerful heart is good medicine."

COLOSSIANS 3:15 (NLT)

"And let the peace that comes from Christ rule in your hearts… And always be thankful."

Our thoughts have a direct impact on our health, so we should be intentional in our thinking. Developing an attitude of gratitude is critical to promoting positive changes in our outlook and overall health. Negative, critical thinking leads to poor health outcomes. Gratitude, however, leads to lower levels of depression and greater life satisfaction.[2] It also retrains our brains to think more positively, which provides further benefit.

Gratitude extends to every area of our lives, whether big or small, material or immaterial. It is not always natural to express our thanks, but it can become a habit through sustained effort.

No matter our circumstances, we can be grateful because of the reality that God's "love endures forever" (Psalm 136:1, NIV). Daily we are given testaments of God's care for us. When we establish a grateful heart in ourselves for the truth of God's abundant love and grace, we begin the transformation of our entire perspective. Whoever we are, whatever we've done, or whatever our outlook may be, we can take comfort in knowing God's love for us is everlasting. As recipients of this gift, we can truly come to Him with singing and "enter his gates with thanksgiving."

Music focused on praise helps prompt gratitude. Listen to the hymn, "Great Is Thy Faithfulness" while meditating on the words. Write your reflection.

Today, start the habit of writing five things you are grateful for each day. Pray, asking God to help you recognize your blessings.

**Reflective Reading:
1 Thessalonians 5:16–18**

DAILY GRATITUDE

1 . . . .
. . . .

2 . . . .
. . . .

3 . . . .
. . . .

4 . . . .
. . . .

5 . . . .
. . . .

MY REFLECTION

Remembering What God Has Done

JOSHUA 4:21–24 (NLT)

"Then Joshua said to the Israelites, 'In the future your children will ask, "What do these stones mean?" Then you can tell them, "This is where the Israelites crossed the Jordan on dry ground." For the Lord your God dried up the river right before your eyes, and he kept it dry until you were all across, just as he did at the Red Sea when he dried it up until we had all crossed over. He did this so all the nations of the earth might know that the Lord's hand is powerful, and so you might fear the Lord your God forever.'"

By nature, we often forget or take for granted the good things that have happened to us. God frequently counseled His people to create memorials of their experiences for this reason. After God appeared to Jacob, Jacob built a pillar, naming it "house of God" as a signifier of God's dwelling presence there with him (Genesis 28:16–19, NLT). When entering into the promised land, the Israelites built a stone memorial to remember the miracles God performed on their behalf to bring them there. These were signs to all who saw them to forever reveal who God is and what He accomplished for His people.

God has never asked us to do something He has not already done Himself: "Can a mother forget her nursing child?... Even if that were possible, I would not forget you! See, I have written your name on the palms of my hands" (Isaiah 49:15, 16, NLT). We remember God because He has remembered us.

While we may gain encouragement from the stories of others, we get the greatest benefit from recalling and sharing our own positive experiences. We may not build pillars, but remembering our experiences is as important for us as it was for those back then. It brings us joy in life and security when times are difficult. It strengthens our faith and trust in God, providing a fuller perspective of His working in our situations. Journaling is a practical way for us to keep track of the things God has done for us. The mere, simple act of writing them down helps us remember. It also helps us develop the habit of being grateful each day.

What has the Lord done for you? Write down a positive experience you have had and what encourages you from it. Pray, asking God to help you remember what He has done for you.

Reflective Reading: Psalm 9, 92, 118

DAILY GRATITUDE

1 . . . .
  . . . .
2 . . . .
  . . . .
3 . . . .
  . . . .
4 . . . .
  . . . .
5 . . . .
  . . . .

MY REFLECTION

Spiritual Hydration

PSALM 63:1 (NKJV)

"O God, You are my God; early will I seek You; my soul thirsts for You; my flesh longs for You in a dry and thirsty land where there is no water."

PSALM 42:1 (NIV)

"As the deer pants for streams of water, so my soul pants for you, my God."

REVELATION 22:17 (NIV)

"The Spirit and the bride say, 'Come!' And let the one who hears say, 'Come!' Let the one who is thirsty come; and let the one who wishes take the free gift of the water of life."

We can survive without food for a few weeks, but we can only live without water for a few days. We know what it is like to be physically thirsty, but have you ever felt a mental or spiritual desire so strongly that it was as a thirst? Just as proper hydration is essential to the functioning of the entire body, so staying hydrated spiritually is vital to maintaining our connection and relationship with God.

Throughout Scripture, water is a metaphor for the Holy Spirit and salvation (Isaiah 12:3, John 7:39). Like water, we need the Holy Spirit and salvation afresh everyday. When Jesus met a woman by a well, He told her that if she wanted, He would give her "living water," which would become in her "a fountain of water springing up into everlasting life" (John 4:10, 14, NKJV). Jesus promised to freely give salvation and the Holy Spirit to her and all who ask. In "drinking" these ourselves, we become a well for others to get this water. Jesus gives such an abundance of salvation and the Holy Spirit it is as "floods on the dry ground" (Isaiah 44:3, NKJV). The Holy Spirit is the abiding presence of God on earth, our Helper, and our means of connecting with God. He dwells within us, teaches us all truth, seals us for redemption, and assures us of our salvation. It is the Holy Spirit who renews and changes us, giving us the results—the fruit—of that change. Without the Holy Spirit, the changes we seek would not be accomplished, and we would quickly die spiritually.

The Holy Spirit is our greatest Helper in our battle with depression and anxiety. He will provide everything our souls are thirsting for. Each time you take a drink of water, remember God's promise.

Are you thirsting spiritually? What does it mean for the Holy Spirit and salvation to be as water? Pray, asking God to give you His Living Water.

> **Reflective Reading: Psalm 42, 107:8, 9; Isaiah 55; John 4, 7:37–39, 14–16; Revelation 21:6**

DAILY GRATITUDE

1 . . . .
. . . .
2 . . . .
. . . .
3 . . . .
. . . .
4 . . . .
. . . .
5 . . . .
. . . .

MY REFLECTION

. . . .

Exercising Faith

1 TIMOTHY 4:8 (NIV)

"For physical training is of some value, but godliness has value for all things, holding promise for both the present life and the life to come."

HEBREWS 11:1 (NLT)

"Faith shows the reality of what we hope for; it is the evidence of things we cannot see."

LUKE 8:48 (NIV)

"Then he [Jesus] said to her, 'Daughter, your faith has healed you. Go in peace.'"

There was a woman who had a flow of blood for 12 years. She had spent her livelihood on physicians and treatments, but all her efforts to get well were futile. When she heard about Jesus and His power to heal, whether through desperation or inspiration she decided to go to Him. She chose to believe He could heal her, even if she only touched His clothing. As Jesus came through her town, she snuck through the crowd, then discreetly touched the hem of His garment. Immediately, she was healed. Jesus sensed power go out of Him. He asked the crowd who had touched Him. Trembling, she came forward. Jesus lovingly commended her faith, calming her fears and giving her emotional healing in addition to the physical healing she had received. She exercised her faith, and it made her well.

Exercise is required to build strength in the body, with daily effort producing long-term gain. In the same way, daily exercising faith strengthens our Christian walk. Faith is the choice to believe God is who He says He is. We exercise it by acting on that belief, like the woman. God has given us precious promises in Scripture; they are ours if we have faith that He will give us what He's promised. We may not receive an immediate answer to our prayers or exactly what we ask for, but we can trust God does hear and will give us what is best for us. Faith will inform the way we respond to what happens in our lives. Instead of worrying about the future, fretting over past mistakes, or struggling to make decisions, through faith we can turn our anxieties over to God, trusting that He saves us, will give us the wisdom and guidance we need, and is helping us through each day as He promised.

How can you exercise faith today? Pray, thanking God for the ways He has helped you in the past and asking Him for faith to get through your struggles.

Reflective Reading: Proverbs 24; Matthew 9:20–22; Luke 8:43–48; Hebrews 11, 12

DAILY GRATITUDE

1 . . . .
. . . .

2 . . . .
. . . .

3 . . . .
. . . .

4 . . . .
. . . .

5 . . . .
. . . .

MY REFLECTION

Reflecting on Scripture

JOSHUA 1:8 (NLT)

"Study this Book of Instruction continually. Meditate on it day and night so you will be sure to obey everything written in it. Only then will you prosper and succeed in all you do."

PROVERBS 3:5–8 (NLT)

"Trust in the Lord with all your heart; do not depend on your own understanding. Seek his will in all you do, and he will show you which path to take. Don't be impressed with your own wisdom. Instead, fear the Lord and turn away from evil. Then you will have healing for your body and strength for your bones."

PSALM 119:105 (NLT)

"Your word is a lamp to guide my feet, and a light for my path."

The words of Scripture contain the beautiful picture of God's ideals for our lives. They are not rigid rules for us to follow, demanding punishments when we break them, but are instead loving instructions from a Creator who knows what will bring the greatest happiness to His creation. While the counsels God has given to us are the best for our well-being, such as sleep, exercise, food, fresh air, sunlight, and water, the words of God themselves bring strength and health. Contemplating and following God's laws provides fresh vim and vigor to our whole person: "The instructions of the Lord are perfect, reviving the soul… The commandments of the Lord are right, bringing joy to the heart. The commands of the Lord are clear, giving insight for living… They are more desirable than gold, even the finest gold. They are sweeter than honey, even honey dripping from the comb" (Psalm 19:7–10, NLT).

God knows the connection between the mind, body, and spirituality. Meditating on Scripture brings our minds to higher themes, elevating our whole being. Studying it increases our intellect and wisdom. No piece of literature can compare in value to God's Word. It brings us healing in every area of life, as well as joy, peace, stability, and security. Consistently spending time in Scripture may be difficult at first, but we build the habit over time. As we contemplate God's Word day and night, our thoughts will influence our actions, and we will see spiritual growth in our deeds and character. The Word of God reveals Jesus, and it is powerful enough to transform us.

What's your favorite verse of Scripture? Why is it your favorite? What does it tell you about Jesus? Write it down, and then reflect on it throughout the day. Pray, asking God to help you spend time daily in His Word.

Reflective Reading: Psalm 19, Proverbs 4, Isaiah 40

DAILY GRATITUDE

1 . . . .
   . . . .

2 . . . .
   . . . .

3 . . . .
   . . . .

4 . . . .
   . . . .

5 . . . .
   . . . .

MY REFLECTION

. . . .
. . . .
. . . .
. . . .
. . . .
. . . .
. . . .
. . . .
. . . .
. . . .

Principles for Reading Scripture

The Bible is full of literary diversity, with stories, laws, histories, poems, songs, letters, visions, prophecies, and revelations. Through it all, it is the Word of God given to humanity. Though an ancient book, it is as much written for us as it was for its original audience. Its principles bridge the gap between us and them, making it relevant to us still today. The Bible requires a close reading—minute details of what is said and how it is said—as well as a broad reading for full interpretation.

The Bible gives us principles for reading it:

- The Scriptures point to Jesus (John 5:39).

- The Bible tells us what is true and what is right and wrong (2 Timothy 3:16).

- The Bible equips us to be better people (2 Timothy 3:17).

- The Scriptures were written to give us hope (Romans 15:4).

- Read one line at a time, comparing Scripture with Scripture (Isaiah 28:10).

- We are to apply the Bible to our lives (2 Timothy 3:14).

Here is a practical study outline we can use when reading the Bible:

- **Pray.** Ask the Holy Spirit to guide you to the truth.

- **What?** What is the original meaning of this passage?

  - What does it actually say? What does it not say? (Sometimes what isn't said is as important as what is).
  - Who is speaking?
  - Who is the Biblical audience? What is the difference between you and them? Do you relate to any of them?
  - What is the historical context? What is the context of the story?
  - Note repetition, lists, contrasts/comparisons, structure, style, key words.

- **So What?** Based on the original meaning, what is the enduring principle? The enduring principle applies across time, cultures, and circumstances. What does this passage tell you about Jesus?

- **Now What?** What is the application to your life? How is God speaking to you through this passage?

This outline can be used if you are reading a single verse, a chapter, or a book. If you don't know where to start, try reading the gospels, biographically (focusing on individuals' stories), cover-to-cover, chronologically, or one book at a time. As you read, don't be afraid to ask questions—you can make them a topic of study. You can also highlight God's promises.

What are your goals for reading Scripture? What questions do you have which you want to study? Pray, asking God to give you the wisdom to understand His Word.

DAILY GRATITUDE

GOALS FOR MY
THINKING AND LIVING

Walking With the Lord

WEEK 2

PRESCRIPTION FOR HEALTH

A SIMPLE DIET WITH A MERRY MIND,
TWO HELPFUL HANDS, A TONGUE THAT'S ALWAYS KIND;
DEEP BREATHING OF PURE AIR—STILL FREE FROM TAX;
WHILE EATING MEALS AND AFTER WORK, RELAX!

TWO SMILING EYES TO PROVE YOU STILL CAN LAUGH;
LIVE SIMPLER LIVES AND CUT YOUR BILLS IN HALF.
A TASK YOU LOVE, A CONSCIENCE CRYSTAL CLEAR;
A HEART AT REST, A MIND THAT'S FREE FROM FEAR.

USE WATER FREELY, MORE WITHIN, WITHOUT;
HAVE FAITH IN GOD AND GIVE NO PLACE TO DOUBT.
THEN EXERCISE YOUR BODY, MIND, AND SOUL;
LOOK UP AND KEEP YOUR EYES UPON LIFE'S GOAL.

———————

Adlai A. Esteb

Read *Telling Yourself the Truth*, chapters 1–3

Prayer, the Breath of the Soul

JAMES 5:15, 16 (NKJV)

"And the prayer of faith will save the sick… Confess your trespasses to one another, and pray for one another, that you may be healed. The effective, fervent prayer of a righteous man avails much."

1 CHRONICLES 16:11 (NLT)

"Search for the Lord and for his strength; continually seek him."

PSALM 150:6 (NLT)

"Let everything that breathes sing praises to the Lord! Praise the Lord!"

Prayer is talking to God, sharing anything on our hearts, whether joys, sorrows, wants, needs, worries, struggles, grievances, etc., for ourselves or another. There is power in prayer: "If you ask anything in My [Jesus'] name, I will do it" (John 14:13, NLT). Praying in faith, we trust that God has the power to help us and intervene in our lives. God certainly hears our prayers: did you know prayer has been scientifically recorded to cure cancer? One study found a prayerful "attitude of devotion and acceptance"— not an aggressive prayer demanding for specific outcomes—led to the spontaneous cure of cancer.[3] An agnostic doctor even concluded that prayer was as essential to healing as strong medication or surgery.

Breathing is a similitude of prayer. Prayer is as vital to our physical and spiritual health as breathing. It is the breath of our hearts, our means of communion with God, the Giver and Source of life. If we lose our connection with Him, we lose our connection with life itself. Prayer lifts us up to God, brings us closer to Him, and allows Him to speak to us. We, through faith, can discern God's nearness to us in prayer. It shows us His love and gives us precious evidence of His care. Through prayer we build a relationship with God, gaining a fuller picture of ourselves and who He is. He becomes our most precious Friend and personal Savior, and we converse with Him as such. Prayer can become as natural to us as breathing.

Prayer is also closely connected with praise. Praise acknowledges God for who He is and expresses our gratitude to Him for what He does for us. It teaches us to be grateful and brings joy to our lives. As we breathe prayers, we should also breathe praise.

While doing deep breathing exercises, open your heart to God as to your friend. Commit to making this your daily routine. Tell God whatever is on your mind and praise Him. Pray, asking God for faith to believe He hears your prayers.

Reflective Reading: Matthew 7:7, 8; Ephesians 3:20; 1 John 5:14, 15

DAILY GRATITUDE

1 . . . .

. . . .

2 . . . .

. . . .

3 . . . .

. . . .

4 . . . .

. . . .

5 . . . .

. . . .

MY REFLECTION

Prayer and Stress

PHILIPPIANS 4:6, 7 (NLT)

"Don't worry about anything; instead, pray about everything. Tell God what you need, and thank him for all he has done. Then you will experience God's peace, which exceeds anything we can understand. His peace will guard your hearts and minds as you live in Christ Jesus."

PSALM 34:17 (NLT)

"The Lord hears his people when they call to him for help. He rescues them from all their troubles."

PSALM 55:22 (NLT)

"Give your burdens to the Lord, and he will take care of you. He will not permit the godly to slip and fall."

When distressing circumstances arise in our lives, we often seek an escape. For many, the escape is seeking a removal of stress or stressors through mind-numbing activities and substances. These coping mechanisms inhibit brain function and reduce rational thinking. As an alternative, both the Bible and research reveal that prayer is a constructive outlet for stress in our lives. Prayer has been shown to increase blood flow to the frontal lobe, the area of the brain responsible for moral reasoning and social behavior, activating it. Prayer also correlates with better mental health and produces positive behaviors.[4] Prayer causes us to apply our minds to and process the stressors we encounter accurately rather than obfuscating the truth for ourselves. The action opens our minds to seeking a higher understanding of and finding solutions for the problems we face, helping us work through them and cope. When practiced consistently, prayer alleviates our stress as well as provides renewed perspective and insight to the circumstances of our lives.

Through prayer, God gives us fortitude to endure life's difficulties: "You will keep in perfect peace all who trust in you, all whose thoughts are fixed on you!" (Isaiah 26:3, NLT). Jesus promises us His Spirit of peace when we pray, trusting Him and looking to Him to take care of all our needs. He is the Truth, and through prayer He will provide the truth we need to have guidance and clarity amidst the stress and difficulties of life.

What strategies do you utilize to cope with the stresses of life? Try prayer as an alternative. Pray, telling God all your struggles and asking for strength and wisdom to persevere through them.

Reflective Reading: Psalm 18:6, 102:17; Lamentations 3:55–58; Luke 12:22–32

DAILY GRATITUDE

1 ....
....
2 ....
....
3 ....
....
4 ....
....
5 ....
....

MY REFLECTION

Persisting in Prayer

EPHESIANS 6:18 (NIV)

"And pray in the Spirit on all occasions with all kinds of prayers and requests. With this in mind, be alert and always keep on praying for all the Lord's people."

LUKE 18:1–8 (NKJV)

"Men always ought to pray and not lose heart… [God] will avenge them speedily."

Elijah, though depressed and anxious, had a powerful prayer life. He prayed for the Israelites to turn from their evil ways to worship God; it happened when he called fire down from heaven. At God's command, he prayed there would be no rain to reveal God's power to king Ahab. After one prayer, there was a complete drought. Three and a half years later, Elijah was directed by God to pray for rain. He prayed, but nothing happened. He prayed a second time, and still nothing. Even though God had told Elijah to pray, Elijah had to persist in prayer, praying seven times until, finally, it poured (1 Kings 17, 18; James 5:16–18).

Sometimes we receive an immediate answer to our prayers and sometimes we do not, even when God wants us to pray and promises to answer our prayers. God is no less willing to hear us because we have to wait for an answer, neither is He more or less persuaded to keep His promise because we persist. It's not that God didn't hear us the first time, but He has us persist in prayer to help us believe He will answer us. God gives us the freedom to choose our path in life. He works with us in our choices when answering His promises, which builds our characters. Prayer gives Him permission to work in our lives, and we should pray until His work in us is completed.

God is ready to answer. Sometimes we do not know what we should pray for, but the Bible promises that "the Spirit himself makes intercession for us" for our needs (Romans 8:26, NLT). Even in our shortcomings, God has made provision for our prayers to be heard. We may not be given everything we ask for or in the way or timing we ask, but we can trust that God hears us and will give us what we need. Cling to His promises! However He answers, He will reveal His power to intervene in our lives and save us.

When has God answered a prayer in your life? When have you had to persist? Commit to praying daily, then see how God intervenes. Pray, asking God for persistence.

Reflective Reading: Exodus 3:7–10; Luke 18:1–8; John 11; 2 Peter 3:9; Revelation 8:3

DAILY GRATITUDE

1 . . . .

. . . .

2 . . . .

. . . .

3 . . . .

. . . .

4 . . . .

. . . .

5 . . . .

. . . .

MY REFLECTION

Connecting With God Through Music

PSALM 147:7 (NIV)

"Sing to the Lord with grateful praise; make music to our God on the harp."

1 SAMUEL 16:23 (NLT)

"Whenever the tormenting spirit from God troubled Saul, David would play the harp. Then Saul would feel better, and the tormenting spirit would go away."

A lot of music has many positive benefits for our brain. Listening to and playing music healthfully stimulates our brains, improving function and aiding in memory. By nature, music is very emotional, and thereby has profound effects on our mood. It influences us to feel the emotions it portrays or exacerbates the emotions we already feel. Thus, it can be useful in the recovery from depression and anxiety.[5]

When Saul rejected God, he began to experience a distressing spirit, causing him anxiety and torment. This spirit was not God's, but an evil spirit as the result of God's Spirit leaving Saul by his choice. Saul's servants noticed his distress. Desiring his recovery, they recommended Saul find a musician to play for him whenever he felt the evil spirit. David was suggested because of his skill on the harp, his looks, his manner, his bravery, and, most importantly, because "the Lord was with him" (1 Samuel 16:18, NLT). When David would play, Saul found relief from the distressing spirit. Listening to the music made him feel better emotionally and physically, with the effects lasting beyond the performance.

Music had a deep impact on Saul's mental, physical, emotional, and spiritual state. But what made the biggest difference was that the Lord was with David. Music is a means of connecting us with God. The heart with which we do something is as important as the action itself—the Lord is worshiped in both spirit and truth. That is why only consecrated people were appointed to be music leaders in the Jewish temple worship service (1 Chronicles 15:16). When we are consecrated to God, He can work through the healing power of music to bring even greater restoration than could come from the music alone. Music is a powerful aid in depression and recovery, but even more powerful is the fact that it brings us into connection with the One best able to give us the recovery we seek.

Try listening to classical music today as you take time to reflect. Select a composer, such as Albinoni, Bach, Beethoven, Brahms, Handel, Mozart, Respighi, Tchaikovsky, or Vivaldi.

Can the Lord be found in the music you're listening to? Pray, asking God to give you a heart for Him and heal you through the music He has given to you.

> **Reflective Reading: 1 Samuel 16:14–23; Ephesians 5:18–20**

DAILY GRATITUDE

1 . . . .

. . . .

2 . . . .

. . . .

3 . . . .

. . . .

4 . . . .

. . . .

5 . . . .

MY REFLECTION

Connecting With God in Nature

PSALM 19:1, 2 (NLT)

"The heavens declare the glory of God. The skies display his craftsmanship. Day after day they continue to speak; night after night they make him known."

PSALM 145:3–5 (NIV)

"Great is the Lord and most worthy of praise; his greatness no one can fathom. One generation commends your works to another; they tell of your mighty acts. They speak of the glorious splendor of your majesty—and I will meditate on your wonderful works."

When God made Adam and Eve, He placed them in a garden for their home, to tend and care for it. Every part of creation, down to the minutest detail, was designed to make them happy. God's love and fatherly care was manifest in each flower, tree, and animal. Fragrant aromas of plants surrounded them, and they were enveloped by the sweet melodies of nature. They daily received fresh air and light in their work, and had the blanket of stars to cover them at night. Continually around them was the beauty of creation to be their delight.

While we may enjoy nature, many of us today spend an enormous amount of time indoors and on devices, which keeps us from participating in activities outside and enjoying the outdoors.

However, spending time in nature has numerous benefits for our health. It gives us fresh air, which clears our lungs of particles of pollution and sickness, as well as improves mood, increases energy, and lowers our heart rates. Spending time in nature reduces stress, decreases depression, and increases cognitive function.[6,7] Walking in its beauty—through woods or fields, listening to the sounds of birds or moving water, noticing patterns and shades of plants—brings recovery to brains overtaxed and anxious.

Though marred with the blight of sin, nature still reveals the creative power and love of its Maker. Nature is our first lesson book, pointing us to the beneficence and care of our Father. It connects us to God and brings us enjoyment. While Jesus was on the earth, He often withdrew into nature to commune with the Father. He also frequently used nature to teach us about God and draw our hearts after Him. As we view our beautiful world, our affections toward God increase and our souls become strengthened and full of energy.

What is your favorite natural landscape? How does nature point your mind to God? Pray, asking God to reveal Himself to you through His created works.

Reflective Reading: Genesis 1, 2; Psalm 95:4, 5

DAILY GRATITUDE

1 . . . .
. . . .

2 . . . .
. . . .

3 . . . .
. . . .

4 . . . .
. . . .

5 . . . .
. . . .

MY REFLECTION

Living in the Light of Life

JOHN 8:12 (NLT)

"Jesus spoke to the people once more and said, 'I am the light of the world. If you follow me, you won't have to walk in darkness, because you will have the light that leads to life.'"

LUKE 11:34–36 (NLT)

"Your eye is like a lamp that provides light for your body. When your eye is healthy, your whole body is filled with light. But when it is unhealthy, your body is filled with darkness. Make sure that the light you think you have is not actually darkness. If you are filled with light, with no dark corners, then your whole life will be radiant, as though a floodlight were filling you with light."

ECCLESIATES 11:7 (NLT)

"Light is sweet; how pleasant to see a new day dawning."

Throughout the Bible, light symbolically represents God's presence. The first thing God created on earth was light, even before the sun. In all their wilderness travel, the Israelites were guided by God through the light enshrouded in the pillar of cloud by day and the pillar of fire by night. In the temple service, a candlestick was always lit. Light rested over the mercy seat in the Most Holy Place of the tabernacle. Whenever God's presence was physically manifested, light was present: on Mount Sinai when God gave the Ten Commandments, at the dedication of Solomon's temple, on the hills of Bethlehem when the angels announced the birth of Christ—to name a few. Jesus spoke of Himself as "the Light of the world," describing His first coming as a light shining in darkness.

Direct sunlight has innumerable benefits for our health, and a lack of it can create negative health issues. We need light spiritually, too. A lack of "light" for our spiritual lives creates the opportunity for darkness—sin and Satan—to gain a foothold. Receiving spiritual light, in God's Word and through the presence of the Holy Spirit, will keep the darkness away. If darkness seems looming, claim the promise that Jesus will shed His light upon us. In receiving light, Jesus said we also become a light for others, pointing them to Him. As light penetrates all the corners of the world, so the light of Christ penetrates our souls, filling our hearts with His love.

Go outside. Notice the light from the sun. What insight does this give you about Christ being the Light of the world? What light have you received from God in your life? Pray, asking God to fill you with His light and make you a light for others.

Reflective Reading: Psalm 18:28; Ecclesiastes 2; Isaiah 60; 1 John 1

DAILY GRATITUDE

1 My friends !

2 Sunshine at the baseball game

3 Watching Kylie play baseball

4 Time to read at night

5 Watching the dogs swim at Lake Sammemish !

MY REFLECTION

Today was a great day. I am happy w/ the time I spent.

Resting in the Lord

EXODUS 33:14 (NIV)

"The Lord replied, 'My Presence will go with you, and I will give you rest.'"

PSALM 127:2 (AMP)

"It is vain for you to rise early, to retire late, to eat the bread of anxious labors—for He gives [blessings] to His beloved even in his sleep."

GENESIS 2:2, 3 (NLT)

"On the seventh day God had finished his work of creation, so he rested. And God blessed the seventh day and declared it holy, because it was the day when he rested from all his work of creation."

In our world today, adequate rest is continually undervalued by the promotion of hustle culture. The stress of overachieving makes it easy to be overworked and taxed to the maximum. Tuning into our body's natural circadian rhythm and providing the brain with rest is crucial to supporting positive health and optimal brain function. God created rest and He created us with a need for it, making it vital to our well-being and intending it to be a blessing. In addition to nightly rest, the Lord created a whole day for physical, mental, and spiritual rest. In speaking of this day, Jesus said, "The Sabbath was made to meet the needs of people, and not people to meet the requirements of the Sabbath" (Mark 2:27, NLT). The Sabbath was created to provide for our needs. It is designed to renew and strengthen our minds and bodies. It gives us the opportunity to spend intentional time in nature and with God, friends, and family. Having this one day a week to rest, be carefree, and be away from our confined and continual work is liberating and restoring.

God gave us this day of rest to ponder Him as our Creator and our Redeemer. He blessed and sanctified the day of rest, not the days of work. He designed to teach us that we are not saved by our work, but through faith and rest in the work of Christ. Christ is our ultimate rest. He is the Provider of our life and salvation. In our world of sin and suffering, He is the One who gives us peace. His peace is found in Himself, and He offers it to all who ask of Him and receive Him.

Reflect on the significance of God creating rest and ordaining it to be a blessing for you. What are your current resting habits? Write one way you plan to physically, mentally, and spiritually rest this week. Pray, asking God to give you His peace and rest.

Reflective Reading: Exodus 20:8–11, 31:13, 17; Deuteronomy 5:12–15

DAILY GRATITUDE

1 . . . .
. . . .

2 . . . .
. . . .

3 . . . .
. . . .

4 . . . .

5 . . . .
. . . .

MY REFLECTION

Principles for a Powerful Prayer Life

Sometimes we don't know how to pray. While Jesus was on the earth, His disciples didn't know either. They asked Him, "Lord, teach us to pray" (Luke 11:1, NKJV). In response, Jesus gave them an outline for prayer, traditionally known as "The Lord's Prayer." This prayer outline can be found in Matthew 6:9–13 and Luke 11:2–4. Study the passages for yourself, then review the principles of prayer:

- Look to God as a loving parent.

- Spend time in intentional gratitude to God for who He is and for all that He has done in and through you.

- Tell God all your needs and the needs of those you are praying for.

- Confess your faults and ask for forgiveness. Forgive others. If you made a mistake, ask God to help you learn from it to turn defeat into victory.

- Ask for the Holy Spirit and deliverance from evil.

Here are some practical prayer tips:

- Talk openly and sincerely to God. Be completely honest with Him, even if you feel you shouldn't. If it helps you stay focused, pray out loud or write down your prayers. Mental focus will make your prayer life more meaningful.

- Claim Bible promises for the situation you or the person you are praying for are in straight from the Scripture. Scripture is the Word of God, so you can expect God to fulfill it. Some promises to start with are:

  - "The Lord is near to all who call upon Him, to all who call upon Him in truth" (Psalm 145:18, NKJV).

  - "When you pass through the waters, I will be with you; and when you pass through the rivers, they will not sweep over you. When you walk through the fire, you will not be burned; the flames will not set you ablaze" (Isaiah 43:2, NIV).

  - "I am the Lord, the God of all mankind. Is anything too hard for me?" (Jeremiah 32:27, NIV).

  - "Call to me and I will answer you and tell you great and unsearchable things you do not know" (Jeremiah 33:3, NIV).

- Ask God to show you if you are following His Word. If you are convicted that you are not following God's instructions, choose to follow Him, asking for the Holy Spirit to keep your commitment and accomplish the work through you.

- Many of the Psalms are prayers, as well as other beautiful songs and poems. Incorporate them into your prayers.

What are victories or answers to prayer you have experienced? Look back to them when you need encouragement. What are your prayer goals this week? Pray, asking God to help you in your prayer life.

DAILY GRATITUDE

GOALS FOR MY
THINKING AND LIVING

Nutrition for the Mind, Body, and Soul

WEEK 3

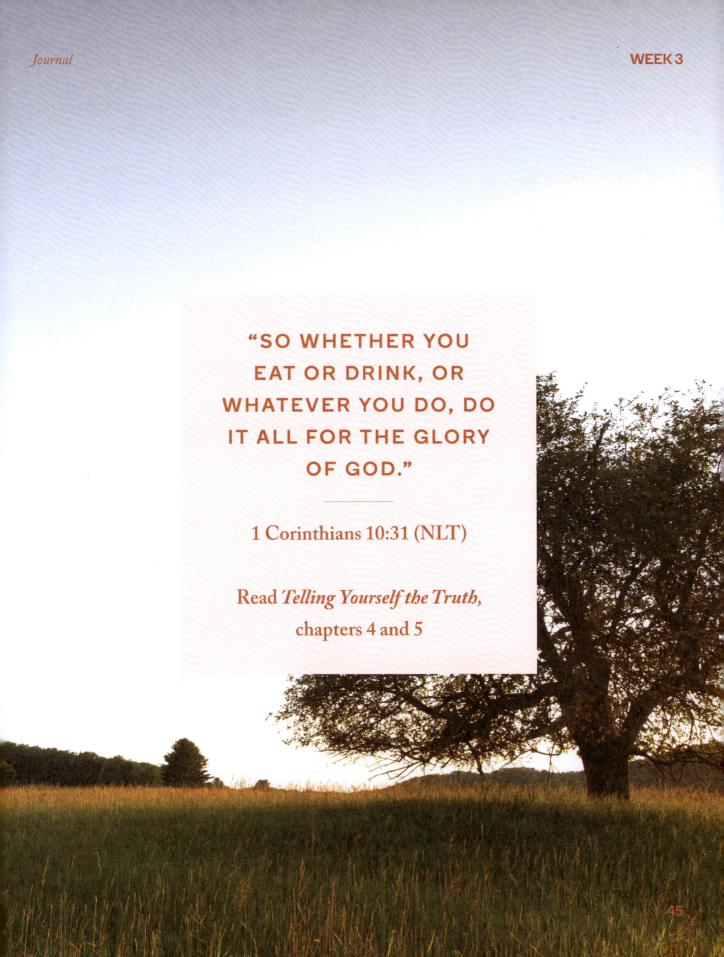

"SO WHETHER YOU
EAT OR DRINK, OR
WHATEVER YOU DO, DO
IT ALL FOR THE GLORY
OF GOD."

———

1 Corinthians 10:31 (NLT)

Read *Telling Yourself the Truth*,
chapters 4 and 5

Of Infinite Value

1 CORINTHIANS 6:19 (NIV)

"Do you not know that your bodies are temples of the Holy Spirit, who is in you, whom you have received from God? You are not your own."

MATTHEW 10:29–31 (NLT)

"Not a single sparrow can fall to the ground without your father knowing it… So don't be afraid; you are more valuable to God than a whole flock of sparrows."

Imagine you saw someone pumping laundry detergent into a car instead of gasoline. What would happen? It wouldn't run, the car would be damaged, and there would probably be lots of bubbles. As we use proper fuel and care for our cars, so should we properly care for ourselves. We are infinitely more valuable than cars. It is more important for us to know how to take care of ourselves than our possessions.

While it is true the cause of a disease may be beyond our control, our lifestyle is frequently a contributing factor. Poor diet, lack of exercise, lack of sleep, etc., compound with other risk factors to put us at greater risk for diseases and hinder our ability to heal from diseases.[8] If lifestyle is a contributing cause of depression and anxiety, why not change it? We may think we are healthy now, so our lifestyle doesn't matter.

Or, we may think it doesn't matter because we will be the ones to suffer the consequences. But these thoughts are not true. Our lifestyle very much affects our current and future health. We are given personal agency, but that does not mean our choices do not affect those around us. The results of our choices touch everyone we come into contact with, our friends and family—those we love and are loved by—being impacted the most. They don't want us or themselves to suffer the negative consequences which come from us not taking care of ourselves.

Jesus paid an infinite price for us by sacrificing Himself on the cross. We are of utmost value to Him. He has given us a great destiny as His sons and daughters. He wants us to be taken care of, be in the best possible condition, and enjoy the blessings of health for the benefit of ourselves and those around us.

What does it mean to be of infinite value to God? How does it affect your life? How does it impact the way you choose to take care of yourself? Pray, asking God for help to see yourself and others the way He does, recognizing the value He has placed on you and them.

Reflective Reading: Isaiah 43:3–7; Matthew 6:25–34; John 1:12; 1 Corinthians 6:20

DAILY GRATITUDE

1 . . . .

. . . .

2 . . . .

. . . .

3 . . . .

. . . .

4 . . . .

. . . .

5 . . . .

. . . .

MY REFLECTION

Spiritual Food

EXODUS 16:4–35 (NLT)

"Then the Lord said to Moses, 'Look, I am going to rain down food from heaven for you. Each day the people can go out and pick up as much food as they need for that day'… And the next morning the area around the camp was wet with dew. When the dew evaporated, a flaky substance as fine as frost blanketed the ground. The Israelites were puzzled when they saw it. 'What is it?' they asked each other… And Moses told them, 'It is the food the Lord has given you to eat'… The Israelites called the food manna… They ate manna until they came to the border of the land of Canaan."

PHILLIPIANS 4:19 (NLT)

"And this same God who takes care of me will supply all your needs from his glorious riches, which have been given to us in Christ Jesus."

The Israelites were frequently moving around in the wilderness after leaving Egypt. Their desert dwelling meant a lack of food. God intervened, daily providing food from heaven to sustain them. The food provided for all their dietary needs and was created to prevent disease (Deuteronomy 7:15). Each morning, the Israelites gathered as much food as they needed for the day, and the remainder would melt in the heat of the day. On Friday, they would pick up a double portion since no manna fell on the Sabbath.

Not only is this a story of God's miraculous provision for His people, but also an allegory of God's spiritual provision for us. As much as we need physical food, we need spiritual food. Jesus refers to Himself as the manna, the "living bread that fell from heaven" (John 6:51, NLT). As the Israelites gathered their daily provision in the mornings, so Jesus wants us to receive our provision of spiritual food each morning through prayer and Bible study to give us the strength and encouragement we need to get through the day. As the manna provided all the needed nutrition for the Israelites, so Christ provides all we need. When we partake of Jesus, He will satisfy all of our spiritual hungerings and we will be saved to live forever with Him. The food is made available to us in more abundance than we could take. Jesus already came down from heaven to make provision for us—we only have to receive Him.

What does it mean for Jesus to provide all of your needs? What are ways you can receive Jesus today? Pray, thanking God for supplying your needs and asking Him to give you spiritual food.

Reflective Reading: Deuteronomy 8:3; Isaiah 50:4; John 6:25–59

DAILY GRATITUDE

1 ....

2 ....

3 ....

4 ....

5 ....

MY REFLECTION

God's Diet Plan

PSALM 32:8 (NLT)

"The Lord says, 'I will guide you along the best pathway for your life. I will advise you and watch over you.'"

GENESIS 1:29 (NLT)

"Then God said, 'Look! I have given you every seed-bearing plant throughout the earth and all the fruit trees for your food.'"

GENESIS 3:18, 19 (NLT)

"It will grow thorns and thistles for you, though you will eat of its grains. By the sweat of your brow will you have food to eat."

ECCLESIASTES 3:13 (NLT)

"And people should eat and drink and enjoy the fruits of their labor, for these are gifts from God."

As a loving Father, God is concerned for our safety. A friend or a family member would advise us to avoid certain traveling routes during bad weather to help us stay safe, so God gives us instructions throughout the Bible to protect us. His guidance is for our benefit and well-being. He does not want us to get hurt, but to have an abundant life in every area.

One such instruction He gives us is diet. The Bible reveals that God's original plan for our diet is whole, plant-based foods. While eating meat was permitted after the flood with certain restrictions, it was never God's original intent for us. A balanced, plant-based diet provides all of the necessary daily vitamins, minerals, and nutrients, leads to lower risk of disease, and contributes to a longer life. Simple, natural plant foods are the most nourishing and healthy, and are the best for our brains. Following this diet, as well as consuming less processed foods, drastically improves our mental health by decreasing depression, anxiety, and fatigue and contributing to greater vitality and life satisfaction.[9–11]

God's diet instructions are not meant to be taxing on us or a sacrifice. Rather, they are given to us for our health and blessing. As our Creator, God knows how to best take care of our bodies. God gave us taste buds and created food to be delicious. He wants us to enjoy our food, but also to by it to have the health to enjoy every other area of our lives.

What are your favorite foods which God has created for you to enjoy? What do you like about them? What are practical ways you can incorporate these healthful foods into your diet? Pray, asking God for help to make healthy food choices.

Reflective Reading: Genesis 2:8–17

DAILY GRATITUDE

1 . . . .

. . . .

2 . . . .

. . . .

3 . . . .

. . . .

4 . . . .

. . . .

5 . . . .

. . . .

MY REFLECTION

From the King's Table

DANIEL 1:5–8 (NLT)

"The king assigned them a daily ration of food and wine from his own kitchens… But Daniel was determined not to defile himself by eating the food and wine given to them by the king."

Daniel and his three friends were kidnapped during the besiegement of Judah by Babylon and exiled to its capital. Scholars estimate that the boys were only about 15 years old. Their homes were destroyed; their families were likely killed. Nebuchadnezzar, the king of Babylon, requested his chief of staff to select healthy, good-looking, and intelligent young men from the noble families of Judah to be taken and trained in the choice Babylonian schools for three years in order for them to join the Babylonian royal service. Daniel and his three friends were selected and brought to the palace. In hopes of giving them a new identity, they were given new, Babylonian names.

At the palace, the king provided the captives food and wine from his personal table. Daniel and his friends immediately recognized they should not eat the food. Firstly, the food was likely offered to Babylonian idols as a part of a religious rite. Secondly, the foods contained unclean meat according to the dietary guidelines given by God (Leviticus 11). Eating these foods would have demonstrated consent to worshiping idols and a disregard for God's laws. Daniel and his friends "determined" to not be defiled—to be faithful to God. Having God-given favor from the chief of staff, Daniel requested he and his friends not eat the king's food but be given vegetables and water instead. He proposed a test: the chief of staff would see for himself if Daniel and his friends or those who ate from the king's table were healthiest after 10 days. The chief of staff was worried it would offend the king, but agreed.

Through their traumatic experience, the boys did not lose their faith in God but were witnesses for Him. The matter of choosing between clean and unclean foods may seem insignificant, but to the Hebrews it was a matter of right and wrong. They knew God's commands and were determined to do what was right, no matter the consequences. They risked their lives to follow God's law and honor Him as their Lord, trusting He would prove Himself to be correct in His instructions.

What is something in your life that you know you need to do, but have been putting off out of fear? How would doing the right thing actually prove most beneficial? Pray, asking God to give you strength to do what is right.

Reflective Reading: Leviticus 11; Deuteronomy 28

DAILY GRATITUDE

1 . . . .
. . . .
2 . . . .
. . . .
3 . . . .
. . . .
4 . . . .
. . . .
5 . . . .
. . . .

MY REFLECTION

Seeking Faithfulness

DANIEL 1:15–20 (NLT)

"At the end of the ten days, Daniel and his three friends looked healthier and better nourished than the young men who had been eating the food assigned by the king. So after that, the attendant fed them only vegetables instead of the food and wine provided for the others. God gave these four young men an unusual aptitude for understanding every aspect of literature and wisdom. And God gave Daniel the special ability to interpret the meanings of visions and dreams… Whenever the king consulted them in any matter requiring wisdom and balanced judgment, he found them ten times more capable than any of the magicians and enchanters in his entire kingdom."

HEBREWS 10:23 (NLT)

"Let us hold tightly without wavering to the hope we affirm, for God can be trusted to keep his promise."

The experiment of Daniel and his friends only eating vegetables and drinking water for 10 days, then comparing their health to others, was the first prospective clinical trial recorded in human history. The four boys were stronger and healthier than the others. From then on, they were given only the diet they requested. Interestingly, science now shows that once a nutrition change is adopted, it takes about seven to ten days for changes to become noticeable. A proper diet improves mood and mental clarity, which is crucial to making good, wise choices. It helps us feel better, improves interpersonal relationships, and contributes to higher-quality social lives.[9] In their decision, the Hebrew boys demonstrated God's laws are not arbitrary but beneficial for health.

These boys revealed steadfastness of character and deep confidence in God through their actions amid trying circumstances. They believed God was faithful, that His law would give them better health, so they took God at His word. God was faithful. He blessed the four Hebrews with wisdom, so much so that the king found them 10 times wiser than anyone else in the kingdom. They were given honor in their earthly position and in the eyes of God. While their diet certainly rewarded their lives with better physical and mental health, it was their faithfulness to God that brought the greatest blessing. God has been faithful to us, and He has called us, through His grace and love, to respond with faithfulness to Him in every area of our lives. As God blessed the Hebrew boys, He will surely bless our faithfulness.

How has God been faithful to you? What is an area of your life in which you feel the conviction to demonstrate faithfulness? Pray, asking God for faithfulness in all things.

Reflective Reading: Deuteronomy 7:9, 31:6; Psalm 25:10, 33:4

DAILY GRATITUDE

1 . . . .

. . . .

2 . . . .

. . . .

3 . . . .

. . . .

4 . . . .

. . . .

5 . . . .

. . . .

MY REFLECTION

Purpose For Fasting

MATTHEW 17:21 (NLT)

"This kind can not be cast off without prayer and fasting."

MATTHEW 6:17, 18 (NLT)

"But when you fast, comb your hair and wash your face. Then no one will notice that you are fasting, except your Father, who knows what you do in private. And your Father, who sees everything, will reward you."

Fasting from food has been shown to provide benefits for our health. It increases the brain-derived neurotrophic factor (BDNF) production which creates neuroplasticity, improving brain function. It establishes ketosis in the body, preparing the brain for positive changes, reduces oxidative damage in the brain, and promotes the production of new brain cells, all of which make us feel better and give us mental clarity.[12-15]

Scripture states that fasting has spiritual purposes. We should always abstain from things harmful to us, but fasting is different in that we temporarily abstain even from good things, whether it is all food, certain foods, technology, or something else. Our fasting should be used to intentionally engage in ministry work and spend more time with God. Jesus counsels that overcoming some spiritual struggles we face or gaining insight into questions we have will require prayer and fasting. Listed are some of the purposes of fasting we find throughout the Bible:

- Showing humility (Psalm 69:10)
- Showing sorrow (2 Samuel 1:12)
- Showing repentance and seeking forgiveness (Jonah 3:7–9)
- Confession of sins (Daniel 9:3–5; Nehemiah 1:4–6)
- Spiritual strength for resisting temptation (Matthew 4:2)
- Obtaining spiritual knowledge, guidance, or clarity (Deuteronomy 9:9–11; 1 Kings 19:8; Acts 9:9)
- Focusing on and strengthening our relationship with God (1 Samuel 1:8–11; Joel 1:13–14)
- Enhancing prayer and supplication (Esther 4:16)
- Praying for the sick (Psalm 35:13)
- Protection and safety (Ezra 8:21)

In each of these examples, fasting is combined with prayer. It focuses our attention on God, the supplier of our needs, and His will, rather than continuing our lives as usual. Our fast demonstrates that we recognize and appeal to God for who He is. We fast when we want to experience a spiritual change, acknowledging only God can accomplish the work of true transformation in our lives.

What spiritual change are you seeking? Is there something you feel called to fast from as you seek this? Pray, asking God to continue His work in you.

Reflective Reading: Isaiah 58

DAILY GRATITUDE

1 . . . .

. . . .

2 . . . .

. . . .

3 . . . .

. . . .

4 . . . .

. . . .

5 . . . .

. . . .

MY REFLECTION

The New Earth

REVELATION 22:1–4 (NLT)

"Then the angel showed me a river with the water of life, clear as crystal, flowing from the throne of God and of the Lamb… On each side of the river grew a tree of life… No longer will there be a curse upon anything. For the throne of God and of the Lamb will be there, and his servants will worship him. And they will see his face, and his name will be written on their foreheads."

ISAIAH 11:6–9 (NLT)

"In that day the wolf and the lamb will live together; the leopard will lie down with the baby goat. The calf and the yearling will be safe with the lion, and a little child will lead them all. The cow will graze near the bear. The cub and the calf will lie down together. The lion will eat hay like a cow. The baby will play safely near the hole of a cobra… Nothing will hurt or destroy in all my holy mountain, for as the waters fill the sea, so the earth will be filled with people who know the Lord."

JOHN 17:3 (NKJV)

"And this is eternal life, that they may know You, the only true God, and Jesus Christ whom You have sent."

When considering what has been provided for us by God here on earth, it is important to look forward to what is to come. God has given us the promise of life eternal in a beautiful new earth. There God's ideal will once again be restored throughout all the universe. The Bible describes it as more glorious than anything we could imagine, painting a picture of peace, tranquility, and community. There will no longer be the marr of sin. No hurt, sorrow, or death will ever be found there. All creatures will live in harmony and for the benefit of others, and all will be sustained by eating from the Tree of Life. We will live in perfection of mind, body, health, and character.

The good news is eternal life can begin for us today. Christ said that eternal life is to know God, to be in a relationship with Him. We can begin a relationship now. Jesus wants to be with us. Heaven will simply be a continuation of the life with Jesus we began here on earth.

Reflect on the future that awaits you in heaven and the new earth. How can you prepare yourself here on earth? What relationship with Jesus do you seek to have now? Pray, asking God for eternal life to begin now through your relationship with Jesus.

Reflective Reading: Isaiah 65:17–25; 2 Corinthians 2:9

DAILY GRATITUDE

1 ....

....

2 ....

....

3 ....

....

4 ....

....

5 ....

....

MY REFLECTION

Principles for Orderliness

PSALM 50:23 (NKJV)

"Whoever offers praise glorifies Me; and to him who orders his conduct aright I will show the salvation of God."

COLOSSIANS 3:23, 24 (NIV)

"Whatever you do, work at it with all your heart, as working for the Lord, not for human masters, since you know that you will receive an inheritance from the Lord as a reward. It is the Lord Christ you are serving."

God is a God of order. At the beginning of creation, He intentionally ordered what He created each day. The world still follows in the order He gave it. When establishing the sanctuary, God ordered each step of the ceremonies, the layout of the camp, and each detail of the designs of the tent. Jesus demonstrated order in His miracles and in the timing of His ministry.

Organization and orderliness, being qualities with which God is concerned, are an important part of managing our lives. As stewards of everything God has given us, we can glorify Him by maintaining structure in our daily lives and managing our affairs well. Doing so also reduces stress, gives us clearer thinking, and provides time for rest and reflection.

Here are some practical principles to help bring order into our lives:

- **Time management.** We manage time to make the most efficient use of it. In our schedules, we make time for our health, rest, devotions, relationships, chores, planning, work, etc. Start managing time by writing down in detail how you spend your time each day. Then, use a planner to schedule your time. Enter your top priorities in the calendar first to ensure they will be given time.

- **Organize your space.** Our space is where we keep ourselves and everything we own. We organize it by putting things away in accordance to their use and the functionality of the space. Everything should be neat and systematically arranged. Choose which space you will organize first. If there is excess clutter or unneeded items, get rid of them.

- **Money management.** In life, we earn and spend money. If we don't keep track, we can create serious problems for ourselves. Create a budget to organize your money. List your income and your *necessary* expenses. Put aside money for savings, tithe, offering, charity, and investing. Then, allocate money for wants.

How can you work with God to better manage your life? Pray, asking for God's guidance and help as you seek to become organized.

Reflective Reading: Psalm 37:23; Proverbs 3, 15, 16; Malachi 3:10–12

DAILY GRATITUDE

GOALS FOR MY
THINKING AND LIVING

The Power of Thinking

WEEK 4

"FINALLY, BROTHERS AND SISTERS, WHATEVER IS TRUE, WHATEVER IS NOBLE, WHATEVER IS RIGHT, WHATEVER IS PURE, WHATEVER IS LOVELY, WHATEVER IS ADMIRABLE —IF ANYTHING IS EXCELLENT OR PRAISEWORTHY— THINK ABOUT SUCH THINGS."

———

Philippians 4:8 (NIV)

Read *Telling Yourself the Truth*, chapters 6–8

Why Is Our Thinking Important?

PSALM 15:1, 2 (NLT)

"Who may worship in your sanctuary, Lord? Who may enter your presence on your holy hill? Those who lead blameless lives and do what is right, speaking the truth from sincere hearts."

ROMANS 12:2 (NLT)

"Don't copy the behavior and customs of this world, but let God transform you into a new person by changing the way you think. Then you will learn to know God's will for you, which is good and pleasing and perfect."

JOHN 8:32 (NLT)

"And you will know the truth, and the truth will set you free."

Have you ever heard the phrase, "you are what you eat?" The Bible goes a step further: "As he thinks in his heart, so is he" (Proverbs 23:7, NKJV). Our thinking has profound effects on our health. While our genetic makeup determines much of who we become, we are also molded greatly by our experiences, environments, and thoughts. Our thoughts physically change our brains, which, in turn, change who we are. As we learn new things or create thinking patterns in life, our brain structure alters, and new neuron connections are formed.[16]

Cognitive distortions are irrational thought patterns which warp our perception of reality and negatively impact who we are. Distorted thinking leads us to stress, depression, anxiety, anger, unnecessary suffering, despair, and failure. Conversely, emotionally intelligent thinking leads us to vitality, peace, joy, empathy, hope, and success. This is why it is important to think correct, accurate thoughts which are clear and rational. Learning our cognitive distortions is the first step to recognizing and changing the way we think, as well as becoming more emotionally intelligent. It will help us readily identify, then correct our thoughts.

When we allow cognitive distortions to lead us, we do not fully realize God's ideal for our lives, making us prone to following the path of sin, shame, and pain. God is the source of all truth, and He desires us to keep our minds on Him, knowing that truth will set us free from the thoughts which enslave us. God wants us to be transformed daily by His renewing of our minds and to speak the truth in our hearts so that we can avoid the pitfalls of distorted thinking to embrace the joyous, abundant life He has for us.

What does it mean to speak the truth in your heart? How does truth provide freedom in your thinking? Pray, asking for God to daily transform your mind to be set free by His truth.

Reflective Reading: John 10:10; Colossians 3:2

DAILY GRATITUDE

1 . . . .
. . . .

2 . . . .
. . . .

3 . . . .
. . . .

4 . . . .
. . . .

5 . . . .
. . . .

MY REFLECTION

Cognitive Behavioral Therapy

JOHN 14:6 (NLT)

"I am the way and the truth and the life."

PROVERBS 4:23–27 (NLT)

"Guard your heart above all else, for it determines the course of your life. Avoid all perverse talk; stay away from corrupt speech. Look straight ahead, and fix your eyes on what lies before you. Mark out a straight path for your feet; stay on the safe path. Don't get sidetracked; keep your feet from following evil."

2 CORINTHIANS 10:5 (NIV)

"We take every thought captive to make it obedient to Christ."

Cognitive behavioral therapy (CBT) provides us the opportunity to improve the ways in which we react to and treat ourselves and others. CBT helps us become aware of our thoughts and beliefs, including cognitive distortions, and learn how to reframe them when needed. It also helps us recognize the interconnection of thoughts, emotions, and behaviors, as well as to be cognizant of our triggers, self-talk, automatic thoughts, and unintentional coping mechanisms. The ultimate goal of CBT is to learn to recognize the truth.[17–22] To implement CBT, we first identify our thoughts. Then, we evaluate our thoughts, labeling any cognitive distortions: does my thinking align with the facts? Is there a problem? What is causing this thought? Is this thought helpful or harmful? Next, we reconstruct and reframe any negative thinking or distortions to further develop positive, rational thoughts.

The Bible gives us a framework for evaluating our thoughts: truth, love, and freedom. Firstly, we must question if our thoughts are true and accurate. Secondly, we must consider if our thoughts are loving toward ourselves and others. Lastly, we must understand if our thoughts promote freedom: do they enslave us to a way of thinking or a certain belief system? Whatever is true will make us free. Each of these principles are associated with the character of Jesus—He is the truth, He is love, and He is freedom—and are promised to be given to us through the Holy Spirit.

Guarding our minds from crooked thinking is a way in which God helps us walk in newness and fullness of life with Him. If we change our thoughts, our emotions and behaviors will naturally change to adjust to them. By aligning our thoughts with God's principles, we can know we are thinking healthy thoughts as God designed.

What does it mean to make every thought obedient to Christ? Pray, asking God to help you recognize the truth as you implement CBT into your life.

Reflective Reading: John 16:13; Hebrews 4:12

DAILY GRATITUDE

1 ....

2 ....

3 ....

4 ....

5 ....

MY REFLECTION

The Most Expensive Bowl of Soup: All or Nothing

GENESIS 25:29–34 (NLT)

"One day when Jacob was cooking some stew, Esau arrived home from the wilderness exhausted and hungry. Esau said to Jacob, 'I'm starved! Give me some of that red stew!' (This is how Esau got his other name, Edom, which means 'red.') 'All right,' Jacob replied, 'but trade me your rights as the firstborn son.' 'Look, I'm dying of starvation!' said Esau. 'What good is my birthright to me now?' But Jacob said, 'First you must swear that your birthright is mine.' So Esau swore an oath, thereby selling all his rights as the firstborn to his brother, Jacob. Then Jacob gave Esau some bread and lentil stew. Esau ate the meal, then got up and left. He showed contempt for his rights as the firstborn."

HEBREWS 12:15–17 (NLT)

"Look after each other so that none of you fails to receive the grace of God. Watch out that no poisonous root of bitterness grows up to trouble you, corrupting many. Make sure that no one is immoral or godless like Esau, who traded his birthright as the firstborn son for a single meal. You know that afterward, when he wanted his father's blessing, he was rejected. It was too late for repentance, even though he begged with bitter tears."

In the story of Jacob and Esau, we see an example of how cognitive distortions can have lasting, unintended consequences. Esau exhibited the all-or-nothing distortion, which is when we have black and white thinking in the extremes. In that moment, the bubbling lentil soup was more important to him than his birthright. His all-or-nothing thought was essentially: "I will die from starvation if I don't eat immediately. What good is my birthright if I'm dead?" Being overcome by dichotomous thinking, he did not hesitate to trade future security, privilege, and blessing for relief from very temporary pain. To him, that single meal was all or nothing for his whole life.

In evaluating this story, the writer of Hebrews states that such extreme thinking, which leads to extreme behavior, is neither good nor God's will for our lives. Emotional intelligence teaches us to recognize the rational truth. There are other options to be sought and evaluated. We should delay our gratification because even though our current situation may feel like life or death, ultimately, things will change and the outcome will be far different than how we originally perceived it with the cognitive distortion.

Have you ever fallen into all-or-nothing thinking? Pray, asking God to help you rationally consider each situation.

Reflective Reading: Isaiah 55:8, 9

DAILY GRATITUDE

1 . . . .

   . . . .

2 . . . .

   . . . .

3 . . . .

   . . . .

4 . . . .

   . . . .

5 . . . .

   . . . .

MY REFLECTION

Our Thoughts and the Truth: Overgeneralization

1 KINGS 19:10–18 (NLT)

"Elijah replied, 'I have zealously served the Lord God Almighty. But the people of Israel have broken their covenant with you, torn down your altars, and killed every one of your prophets. I am the only one left, and now they are trying to kill me, too…' 'Yet I will preserve 7,000 others in Israel who have never bowed down to Baal or kissed him!'"

PSALM 73:5, 17 (NLT)

"[The wicked] don't have troubles like other people; they're not plagued with problems like everyone else… Then I went into your sanctuary, O God, and I finally understood the destiny of the wicked."

Overgeneralization is the cognitive distortion of basing our beliefs on broad suppositions which have limited factual evidence. It severely hinders our ability to base our beliefs on the truth because it causes us to think our assumptions are the truth. The incorrect beliefs then cause us to think there is only one course of action. It frequently uses "always" or "never" statements, but it doesn't necessitate them.

The prophet Elijah struggled with overgeneralization. Jezebel had killed many prophets of God and wanted Elijah dead. This alone prompted Elijah to presume he was the only one faithful alive. The weight of his emotions caused him to believe death was his only possible destiny. His conclusion was based on little evidence. God corrected Elijah's distortion: he was not the only one left, but there were 7,000 faithful people in Israel. The psalmist Asaph also struggled with this distortion. He saw good things happen to wicked people, yet he was honoring God but struggling daily. He assumed they had no share of life's problems and a grand future ahead of them, but he would continually suffer strife. He couldn't see past his limited experience. When Asaph went to God with his concern, he saw the real picture: the wicked will be destroyed, but God had saved him and was strengthening his heart (Psalm 75:19, 26). "I was so foolish and ignorant," he said, once he realized the truth (v. 22).

To overcome overgeneralization, we have to ask ourselves if we have actual evidence to support our ideas. Even when we don't know the truth, we can reach out to the One who does. He will reveal the truth to us in the face of our volatile emotions.

What overgeneralizations do you believe? Reframe your assumptions to match the truth. Pray, asking God to help you identify overgeneralized thoughts before they turn into beliefs.

Reflective Reading: Psalm 25:5, 73

DAILY GRATITUDE

1 . . . .

 . . . .

2 . . . .

 . . . .

3 . . . .

 . . . .

4 . . . .

 . . . .

5 . . . .

 . . . .

MY REFLECTION

. . . .

. . . .

. . . .

. . . .

. . . .

. . . .

. . . .

. . . .

. . . .

. . . .

. . . .

. . . .

. . . .

Can Anything Good Come From Nazareth? Mental Filters

JOHN 1:45, 46 (NLT)

"'Nazareth!' exclaimed Nathanael. 'Can anything good come from Nazareth?' 'Come and see for yourself,' Philip replied."

Our mental filters have profound effects on the way we handle and perceive the situations in life. The mental filter distortion occurs when we single out one component of something to the exclusion of all others. It causes us to react, not respond. Mental filters are created by our core beliefs and experiences, and through them we interpret everything.

When Nathanael heard the One who was foretold by Moses and the prophets was from Nazareth, he didn't believe it. His prejudice against Nazarenes created a mental filter: he focused on Jesus being from Nazareth, disregarding everything else, and thus made a poor assumption as to who Jesus was. His friend Philip encouraged him to consider an alternative by seeing for himself if the other facts about Jesus mattered. Nathanael agreed, then went to meet Jesus. When Jesus saw Nathanael coming to meet Him, He spoke to Nathanael as if He knew him. Nathanael wondered how Jesus could know him since they hadn't met before. Jesus responded by telling him that He had seen him under the fig tree. Nathanael knew he had been under the tree alone—no one could have seen him there. He then realized who Jesus was. He saw the other facts did matter, recognizing he had been wrong in his thinking. His heart changed and his mental filter was corrected.

With mental filters, we don't allow ourselves to see the whole picture. They often cause us to see others in an incorrect, negative light. They teach us to rely wholly upon our feelings to the exclusion of faith and reason. Jesus doesn't want us to create mental filters, but to be willing to look for the true picture and assume the best about others until proven wrong. He is willing to reveal His perspective to teach us to trust Him in every situation. He will help us evaluate our thoughts to give us the power to overcome mental filters. In overcoming this distortion, our core beliefs can become based on Scripture and our thinking can respond in faith.

When have you experienced the mental filter distortion? Pray, asking God to help you see the truth clearly.

Reflective Reading: Proverbs 12:15; Jeremiah 17:7, 8; John 1:45–51

DAILY GRATITUDE

1 . . . .
  . . . .
2 . . . .
  . . . .
3 . . . .
  . . . .
4 . . . .
  . . . .
5 . . . .
  . . . .

MY REFLECTION

A Look at the Heart: Mind Reading

1 SAMUEL 16:6, 7 (NLT)

"When they arrived, Samuel took one look at Eliab and thought, 'Surely this is the Lord's anointed!' But the Lord said to Samuel, 'Don't judge by his appearance or height, for I have rejected him. The Lord doesn't see things the way you see them. People judge by outward appearance, but the Lord looks at the heart.'"

Many of us often engage in the mind reading cognitive distortion with confidence! It is believing we know what someone else is thinking without asking them. It can have drastic consequences in our lives by ruining good relationships, causing unnecessary pain, or inspiring incorrect courses of action, among other things.

Samuel the prophet was sent by God to the household of Jesse to select and anoint the next king of Israel. Jesse brought his sons before Samuel to be presented to him one by one. As soon as Samuel saw the eldest, tallest, and strongest son, he assumed he would surely be God's choice. God immediately corrected Samuel's supposition by telling him what He actually thought. He called out Samuel's distortion, reminding him that he can only see the outside. It is God alone who can read minds. Samuel did not make the same mistake twice.

He waited for the Lord to tell him which of the men would be the next king. The Lord chose David, whom we know as the most famous and powerful king in all of Israel's history. If Samuel had trusted his ability to read God's mind, much of what we know about history and Scripture would be completely different.

As we can't read God's mind, we can't read the minds of others. If we know people cannot read our minds, why would we think we can read theirs? It is true that people may try to conceal their true feelings, and while we may sense they're hiding something, even then we cannot assume we know what they are thinking. As Samuel learned to ask God what He thinks, we too need to learn to ask God and others what their thoughts are. We must avoid making assumptions about what others are thinking and evaluate the facts we do know. All we can see is the outward appearance, and we have to trust God to look upon the heart.

Have you ever assumed you knew what God wanted without asking? What about others? How can you avoid trying to read the minds of others? Pray, asking God to reveal His thoughts to you through the Holy Spirit and His Word.

Reflective Reading: 1 Corinthians 2:10–16

DAILY GRATITUDE

1 . . . .
   . . . .

2 . . . .
   . . . .

3 . . . .
   . . . .

4 . . . .
   . . . .

5 . . . .
   . . . .

MY REFLECTION

Seeing the Future: Fortune Telling

ECCLESIASTES 8:7 (NLT)

"Since no one knows the future, who can tell someone else what is to come?"

GENESIS 12:13 (NLT)

"So please tell them you are my sister. Then they will spare my life and treat me well because of their interest in you."

NUMBERS 13:31 (NLT)

"But the other men who had explored the land with him disagreed. 'We can't go up against them! They are stronger than we are!'"

Even though we know no one can see the future, many still engage in the cognitive distortion of fortune telling. We often fortune tell in an effort to emotionally prepare for what we perceive lies ahead. It's different from assessing the consequences of our choices because it assumes we can predict the outcome of an event without a real consideration of the facts. Our predictions can feel so real—as if they've already happened—that we don't doubt them as we would someone who claims to predict the future. However, the emotions we experience and conclusions we come to through this distortion are not based on truth.

Abram was certain the Egyptians would kill him so they could take his wife. Out of fear, he told her to tell them she was his sister. Believing their lie, Pharaoh took her to marry her. Abram supposed he judged right until God intervened, revealing to Pharaoh the truth. Pharaoh rebuked Abram for his lie and for allowing him to sin by taking his wife, proving Abram's fortune telling wrong. Moses sent 12 Israelite spies to scout the land of Canaan. Ten of them came back with a negative report, convincing the Israelites that the inhabitants of the land were too strong for them to overtake. While this may seem a reasonable concern, it was fortune telling because God had promised the land to Israel at that time. Because of their unbelief in God's promises, they spent 40 years in the wilderness before entering Canaan.

God alone knows the future. All we can know about it is that God will keep His word. Therefore, we ought to train our minds to focus on what God says. In believing our fortune telling, we keep ourselves from obtaining the blessings He has for us. We may be afraid of reality or not knowing what's ahead, but we can trust the One who does know the future to lead us through.

What was a time you found yourself fortune telling? What really happened? Reflect on the results of fortune telling versus trusting God. Pray, asking God for faith to trust Him for the future.

Reflective Reading: Genesis 12:10–20; Numbers 13, 14

DAILY GRATITUDE

1 . . . .
. . . .

2 . . . .
. . . .

3 . . . .
. . . .

4 . . . .
. . . .

5 . . . .
. . . .

MY REFLECTION

. . . .
. . . .
. . . .
. . . .
. . . .
. . . .
. . . .
. . . .
. . . .
. . . .

Principles for Overcoming the Struggles of Our Minds

PSALM 103:13, 14 (NLT)

"The Lord is like a father to his children, tender and compassionate to those who fear him. For he knows how weak we are; he remembers we are only dust."

EPHESIANS 4:23 (NLT)

"Let the Spirit renew your thoughts and attitudes."

In our battle to overcome depression and anxiety, we may find our thoughts are frequently our greatest hindrance. We often have had cognitive distortions or critical, negative thinking in our thought patterns for so long that they have become natural to our thinking, making it difficult to recognize and change them.

Here's the good news: we are not the enemy. The devil is the enemy. He is the one who tempts us to irrational thinking. Our desire often isn't to have cognitive distortions or to be critical, but to cope with and process the struggles of life. This desire is normal and healthy. In the moment of desperation to cope we may be tempted to fall into distorted and negative patterns of thinking, but God has provided us another way.

The truth of Christ has made us completely free. The Holy Spirit can change our thinking if we let Him, and through Him we have the power to make positive choices. We can claim the promise that God has changed our hearts, and when we are struggling to see it, we can claim the promise that God is greater than our hearts (Ezekiel 36:26; 1 John 3:20). We can believe even when we do not feel it because God has promised (2 Corinthians 5:7).

God does not condemn us for struggling with our distortions or temptations to sin. We are His children created in His image, deeply loved by Him and precious in His sight. That's how He sees us. He knows the weakness of our frame and He has compassion on us. He wants us to come to a knowledge and recognition of the truth for our own health and benefit. In optimizing our thinking, we optimize our health. We have the steps of cognitive behavioral therapy we can follow and, thankfully, God is the best therapist. He has promised to complete His perfect work in us (Philippians 1:6).

What thoughts do you have which are contrary to God's ideal for your life? Write out your beliefs based on cognitive distortions, then write a Bible verse telling you the truth. Pray, asking God to change your thinking habits to be healthy and truthful.

DAILY GRATITUDE

GOALS FOR MY
THINKING AND LIVING

Thinking to Heal

WEEK 5

GOD, GRANT ME THE SERENITY

TO ACCEPT THE THINGS I CANNOT CHANGE;

COURAGE TO CHANGE THE THINGS I CAN;

AND WISDOM TO KNOW THE DIFFERENCE.

LIVING ONE DAY AT A TIME;

ENJOYING ONE MOMENT AT A TIME;

ACCEPTING HARDSHIPS AS THE PATHWAY TO PEACE.

TAKING, AS HE DID, THIS SINFUL WORLD AS IT IS,

NOT AS I WOULD HAVE IT.

TRUSTING THAT HE WILL MAKE ALL THINGS RIGHT

IF I SURRENDER TO HIS WILL.

THAT I MAY BE REASONABLY HAPPY IN THIS LIFE,

AND SUPREMELY HAPPY WITH HIM FOREVER IN THE NEXT.

AMEN.

UNKNOWN

Read *Telling Yourself the Truth*, chapters 9 and 10

The Slippery Slope: Emotional Reasoning

ECCLESIASTES 8:11 (NLT)

"When a crime is not punished quickly, people feel it is safe to do wrong."

Have you ever tried running down a steep slope? You may have begun at a slow pace, but as your momentum grew and gravity took over, each step was quicker and each stride longer than the one before, causing you to accelerate through the end of the hill. A similar phenomenon occurs when we disobey God's instructions. Our initial steps may seem slow and small, but each one becomes quicker, bigger, and easier the more we go down the slope of sin.

Ecclesiastes states that when there are no immediate consequences for sinful behavior we may consider that behavior to be harmless or even desirable, and we often continue in it. Our actions will begin to be based on our feelings rather than what is right and wrong, then our feelings may become the basis upon which we decide what is right and wrong. Such thinking is the cognitive distortion called emotional reasoning. Emotional reasoning can best be described as thinking your feelings don't, or perhaps even can't, lie. With this distortion, when something feels right to us, we conclude it must be right, even if we logically know otherwise.

Solomon ran down the slope of sin and into emotional reasoning, leading to a miserable life. God outlined specific guidelines for the king in His law (Deuteronomy 17:14–17). Solomon defied all these commandments. He abused his authority by amassing horses, gold, and silver for himself from his people. He married pharaoh's daughter, an unbeliever, then married many more foreign women, obtaining 1,000 wives and concubines in total. He joined his pagan wives in worshiping their false gods, leading his kingdom to do the same. He felt he loved these women, so he emotionally reasoned his choices must be acceptable, continuing to run down the slope. When Solomon returned to God later in his life, he looked back and processed his bad choices. He declared "it was all so meaningless" (Ecclesiastes 2:11, NLT).

Our only safety from falling into the trap of emotional reasoning is to diligently obey God and trust in His Word. No matter how far down the slope of sin we have run, we can still turn back to Jesus. God will help anybody who wants to come to Him and learn how to think correctly.

What was a time you used emotional reasoning? Pray, asking God to help you base your beliefs, thoughts, and actions on His Word.

Reflective Reading: Numbers 20:1–13; Ezekiel 33:11; John 6:37

DAILY GRATITUDE

1
2
3
4
5

MY REFLECTION

When Facing a Giant: Magnification and Minimization

1 SAMUEL 17:32–47 (NLT)

"'Don't worry about this Philistine,' David told Saul. 'I'll go fight him!… The Lord who rescued me from the claws of the lion and the bear will rescue me from this Philistine!'… David replied to the Philistine, 'You come to me with sword, spear, and javelin, but I come to you in the name of the Lord of Heaven's Armies—the God of the armies of Israel, whom you have defied… Everyone assembled here will know that the Lord rescues his people, but not with sword and spear. This is the Lord's battle, and he will give you to us.'"

ISAIAH 41:10 (NLT)

"Don't be afraid, for I am with you. Don't be discouraged, for I am your God. I will strengthen you and help you. I will hold you up with my victorious right hand."

David and Goliath is a poignant illustration of the magnification and minimization cognitive distortion. The Philistines waged war with Israel, presenting their champion, Goliath. When king Saul and the Isrealites first saw him, they froze in fear. They focused only on Goliath's threat, allowing it to magnify in their minds, and minimized the truth that they were under God's protection as His chosen people. When David entered the camp, he heard Goliath's taunt. He reminded the soldiers of the truth, asking, "Who is this pagan Philistine anyway, that he is allowed to defy the armies of the living God?" (1 Samuel 17:26, NLT). Goliath was nothing compared to God. David offered to fight the giant. Saul viewed David as too young and inexperienced, minimizing his abilities. David insisted that God would keep His promise to Israel and save him from Goliath, neither magnifying nor minimizing his own strength. When David went to meet the Philistine, Goliath mocked him, minimizing his competence as a warrior, thereby minimizing God. David spoke the truth and claimed God's victory, then slew the giant.

David's key to avoiding magnification and minimization was letting faith inform his thinking. He believed God and acted upon the truth of His Word. Our perspective is balanced when it is based on truth. We too have giants to fight in our lives. We are in the Lord's battle; He will fight for us and give us the victory. Our problems are not too great for God. He values us so much that Jesus died to save us. By internalizing truth, faith will inform our thinking.

Have you ever magnified or minimized a problem? How can you instead have a balanced perspective? Pray, asking God for faith to inform your thinking.

Reflective Reading: Numbers 23:19; 1 Samuel 17

DAILY GRATITUDE

1 . . . .

. . . .

2 . . . .

. . . .

3 . . . .

. . . .

4 . . . .

. . . .

5 . . . .

. . . .

MY REFLECTION

Viewing Yourself: Personalization

1 SAMUEL 8:7 (NLT)

"'Do everything they say to you,' the Lord replied, 'for they are rejecting me, not you. They don't want me to be their king any longer.'"

LUKE 9:53–55 (NLT)

"But the people of the village did not welcome Jesus because he was on his way to Jerusalem. When James and John saw this, they said to Jesus, 'Lord, should we call down fire from heaven to burn them up?' But Jesus turned and rebuked them."

The personalization cognitive distortion is a pattern of thinking which assumes total responsibility on ourselves or another for situations we or they have little or nothing to do with, whether positive or negative. This distortion causes us to take an outsized view of how the situations we find ourselves in relate to us and to have an unwarrantedly harsh reaction toward ourselves and others. As a result, personalization is detrimental to our actions, relationships, and self-image.

The Isrealites rejected God's theocratic government and sought for a king to lead them. As God's representative to the people, Samuel was saddened at their request and felt they had rejected him. He blamed himself even though he had faithfully served God. God reminded Samuel

that the people rejected God as their leader, not him. Shortly before Jesus' death, He and His disciples were passing through a Samaritan village on their way to Jerusalem. Because Jesus wasn't planning to stay with them, they rejected Him. The disciples took personal offense to this, feeling targeted by the Samaritans. They fully blamed the Samaritans for their feelings, so they thought the village should be destroyed. They assumed Jesus would agree with them, but He rebuked them for having the wrong spirit in the situation.

Samuel's personalization led to feelings of false personal responsibility for a lack of faithfulness by God's people. The disciples' personalization also led to feelings of rejection, but they put the responsibility on others. God corrected each instance of the distorted thinking. God is the Defender and Rewarder of His people. He does not desire us to take or place incorrect responsibility. We can ask ourselves: am I actually in control of this situation? Am I actually responsible? What is actually being rejected in this situation? Answering these questions will help us understand the truth of the matter.

In what areas of your life do you struggle with personalization? What do you think caused that personalization? Pray, asking God to help you correctly view yourself and others in each situation.

Reflective Reading: Deuteronomy 32:4; 1 Samuel 8

DAILY GRATITUDE

1 . . . .

. . . .

2 . . . .

. . . .

3 . . . .

. . . .

4 . . . .

. . . .

5 . . . .

. . . .

MY REFLECTION

In the Eyes of God: Mislabeling

JOHN 4:9 (NLT)

"The woman was surprised, for Jews refuse to have anything to do with Samaritans. She said to Jesus, 'You are a Jew, and I am a Samaritan woman. Why are you asking me for a drink?'"

JOHN 9:2, 3 (NLT)

"'Rabbi,' his disciples asked him, 'why was this man born blind? Was it because of his own sins or his parents' sins?' 'It was not because of his sins or his parents' sins,' Jesus answered. 'This happened so the power of God could be seen in him.'"

Mislabeling is the cognitive distortion where we attach a label to ourselves or someone else based on insufficient evidence, misconstruing our perception and perverting what we believe to be truth. It's easy to fall into because it allows us a shortcut to conclusions instead of having to think critically about the emotions, situations, and people we encounter. When we continually rehearse and apply labels, we reinforce false perspectives.

In Jesus' day, the Jews had labeled the Samaritans as less-than and outside the promise of the Messiah, so they had no dealings with them. When encountering the Samaritan woman at the well, Jesus disregarded the labels of Jew and Samaritan by asking the woman for a drink.

Startled, the women rehearsed how society taught He should be treating her, even mentioning the contentions between the people groups. Jesus then broke down these labels one-by-one, taught her the truth in connection to what she knew, and offered her salvation. The Messiah, thought unavailable to her by labels, had Himself come to save her. It was only by discarding the labels that Jesus was able to minister to her.

The man blinded from birth had been labeled as unworthy, the recipient of punishment for some sin. The disciples, believing the label, wanted to clarify whose sin the man was being punished for. Jesus corrected and dismantled their label: the man's blindness was not a punishment for any sin. Rather, his blindness was a result of living in a sinful world. God ordained that Jesus would reveal the power of God through his life. The man thought unworthy by the Jews received the privilege of a personal miracle from God Himself.

Our safeguard against mislabeling is to examine the evidence, thinking critically about it and taking truth at face value. Jesus wants us to see ourselves and others as He does—children of our Heavenly Father.

What labels do you ascribe to God, church, yourself, and others? How do they compare to the truth proclaimed by Christ? Pray, asking God to help you see others and yourself as He sees them and you.

Reflective Reading: Psalm 139:17, 18; John 4, 9; Ephesians 1:5; 1 John 3:1, 2

DAILY GRATITUDE

1 ....
....
2 ....
....
3 ....
....
4 ....
....
5 ....
....

MY REFLECTION

The Validity of Truth: Disqualifying the Positive

EXODUS 16:2, 3 (NLT)

"There, too, the whole community of Israel complained about Moses and Aaron. 'If only the Lord had killed us back in Egypt,' they moaned. 'There we sat around pots filled with meat and ate all the bread we wanted. But now you have brought us into this wilderness to starve us all to death.'"

PSALMS 78:40–42 (NLT)

"Oh, how often they rebelled against him in the wilderness and grieved his heart in that dry wasteland. Again and again they tested God's patience and provoked the Holy One of Israel. They did not remember his power and how he rescued them from their enemies."

The disqualifying the positive cognitive distortion occurs when we acknowledge the good but, in pseudo-objectivity, preclude all its value. It can be difficult to notice at first because we may appear to be reasonable in our perception by recognizing both good and bad. However, it eliminates all possibility for anything positive to occur in our lives by discrediting everything that is good. It dismisses good as luck or undeserved kindness or as something so easy it "doesn't count."

When the Israelites were led by God in the wilderness, they frequently fell into this distortion. Within a couple of months, they saw God bring numerous plagues on the Egyptians, deliver them from their enslavers, part the sea and swallow the Egyptians in it, lead them with His visible presence in a pillar of fire by day and cloud by night, and even make bitter waters drinkable. Yet, they discounted these miracles as soon as they felt a need. They complained, claiming the Lord wanted their demise. They didn't consider that He would provide for them as He had their whole sojourn. They disqualified the positive each time they encountered a hardship or discomfort, inhibiting themselves from celebrating the miracles God accomplished for them.

When we disqualify the positive, we allow feelings and fears to dominate over truth and deny its validity. God wants us to enjoy the blessings He gives us in life. He is a Giver of good things. The only way to overcome disqualifying the positive is to tediously give credit to the good and be grateful, aligning our thinking with the truth.

What good things in your life do you frequently reject? How would believing the truth impact you? Pray, asking God to help you recognize the good.

Reflective Reading: Matthew 7:11; James 1:17

DAILY GRATITUDE

1 ....

2 ....

3 ....

4 ....

5 ....

MY REFLECTION

Coping With Life's Stressors

2 CORINTHIANS 12:9, 10 (NLT)

"Each time he said, 'My grace is all you need. My power works best in weakness'… That's why I take pleasure in my weaknesses, and in the insults, hardships, persecutions, and troubles that I suffer for Christ. For when I am weak, then I am strong."

As humans living in a sinful world, we deal with various forms of stress. Sometimes stress can be positive, but prolonged stress poses risks to our health. Cognitive distortions are just one type of internal stressor, and one which we can control. However, throughout our lives we will go through many external, stressful struggles and negative experiences beyond our control. If not dealt with, the stress can lead to bitterness, anger, or resentment, which shackle our thinking and lead to a miserable life. The apostle Paul went through numerous traumatic, stressful experiences during his life:

"Five different times the Jewish leaders gave me thirty-nine lashes. Three times I was beaten with rods. Once I was stoned. Three times I was shipwrecked. Once I spent a whole night and a day adrift at sea. I have traveled on many long journeys. I have faced danger from rivers and from robbers. I have faced danger from my own people, the Jews, as well as from the Gentiles. I have faced danger in the cities, in the deserts, and on the seas. And I have faced danger from men who claim to be believers but are not. I have worked hard and long, enduring many sleepless nights. I have been hungry and thirsty and have often gone without food. I have shivered in the cold, without enough clothing to keep me warm" (2 Corinthians 11:24–27, NLT).

Even with the plethora of hardships, Paul was not bitter. He never lost his faith in God, and came through stronger than before. Paul's key to emerging from stress was healthy coping strategies. He recognized that many of his trials were persecutions for his faith. He trusted that God had not abandoned him and believed in the grace of God to be sufficient for him.

In order to healthfully cope, we must learn to identify and process our stressors and their causes. Then, we can act to eliminate and manage our stressors. This can be a difficult task, but Christ promises that His strength will be sufficient for us. Through Christ, we too can cope with life's stressors.

What are some stressors in your life right now? How can you lean on the strength of Christ to persevere? Pray, asking God to give you grace sufficient for your needs.

Reflective Reading: Isaiah 43:2; John 16:16–33; 2 Corinthians 4:8–18; Philippians 4:19

DAILY GRATITUDE

1 . . . .

. . . .

2 . . . .

. . . .

3 . . . .

. . . .

4 . . . .

. . . .

5 . . . .

. . . .

MY REFLECTION

Forgiveness

EPHESIANS 4:31, 32 (NLT)

"Get rid of all bitterness, rage, anger, harsh words, and slander, as well as all types of evil behavior. Instead, be kind to each other, tenderhearted, forgiving one another, just as God through Christ has forgiven you."

Forgiveness is releasing our resentment and offering something positive for someone who has harmed us, whether or not they deserve it.[23] It acknowledges the action against us was wrong and unacceptable—we don't forgive people because what they did was right. It gives us more empathy for others, even those who hurt us, but doesn't release them from the accountability of their actions or mean we trust them again. Forgiveness is a choice—the feelings of forgiveness come later in time.

Jonah, a prophet, struggled with forgiveness. The Lord called Jonah to go to Nineveh, the Assyrian capital city infamous for extreme wickedness and cruelty, to preach God's impending judgment upon it. Jonah initially ran away from his calling, but after a series of events, he obeyed. Jonah walked the entire city, proclaiming it would be destroyed in 40 days. The whole city believed God's message and repented. They fasted, put on garments for mourning, and prayed to God that He would save them. God saw their repentance, heard their prayers, and saved them.

God's mercy toward Nineveh made Jonah angry. He complained to God: "Didn't I say before I left home that you would do this, Lord?... I knew that you are a merciful and compassionate God, slow to get angry and filled with unfailing love" (Jonah 4:2, NLT). Jonah was bitter and prideful, not forgiving toward those whom God had forgiven. He wanted to see the destruction he predicted come to pass, wishing he would die if it didn't. As Jonah watched the city to see its fate, God tried to reason with him, giving him cognitive behavioral therapy for his negative thoughts and feelings. He left Jonah with this: "Nineveh has more than 120,000 people living in spiritual darkness... shouldn't I feel sorry for such a great city?" (Jonah 4:11, NLT). The story ends there. We don't know how Jonah responded to God's questions. The response to God's call to forgive is up to us.

Forgiveness gives you the power to not let your pain define you. It is about you, not those who hurt you. God will avenge the wrong done to you. He desires you to live in freedom, not enslaved to your wounds.

What bitterness are you holding in your heart that God is calling you to forgive? Pray, asking God to give you forgiveness and the freedom that comes with it.

Reflective Reading: Genesis 50:19–21; Deuteronomy 32:35, 36; Jonah

DAILY GRATITUDE

1

2

3

4

5

MY REFLECTION

Principles for Forgiveness

Whether we realize it or not, a lack of forgiveness is detrimental to our health. The harbored anger, bitterness, and hatred increase chronic stress, heart disease, diabetes, high blood pressure, depression, and anxiety, as well as lower immune response, damage new relationships, and keep us from enjoying the present. Forgiveness does the exact opposite. It also improves sleep, lowers cholesterol, and decreases the amount of physical pain we feel. It cancels out the effects of lifetime stress, producing positive health.[24-26] Forgiveness does not preclude justice or accountability, but it lets go of resentment, allowing us to take full control of our lives. Forgiveness doesn't equal trust—trust is earned. When someone proves untrustworthy, we shouldn't trust them.

When we've carried resentment for years, it can be difficult to know what forgiveness looks like or how to accomplish it. The truth is, when someone has deeply hurt us, we do not have it in ourselves to forgive. Forgiveness is made possible only by the grace of Christ. It can be a long, arduous process, but Christ gives strength for each step. He promises forgiveness will help heal us. He will give us the restoration we seek.

We have to ask God for forgiveness through prayer.

- Pray for yourself. Be fully honest with God about how you are feeling. Pray you will no longer be adversely affected by what has happened to you. Pray for healing.

- Pray for forgiveness. Pray for the strength to choose forgiveness, to keep the commitment of your choice, and for emotional forgiveness.

- Pray for those who hurt you to change to no longer hurt others.

Jesus was beaten and abused, oppressed and despised. Though He had done no wrong, He was condemned to the cruelest of deaths. While Jesus was on the cross, speaking of those who put Him there, He said, "Father, forgive them, for they don't know what they're doing" (Luke 23:34, NLT). He acknowledged what happened to Him and prayed, asking God's forgiveness for His abusers. Jesus has forgiven us for the sins that nailed Him to the cross. He wants us to experience freedom and healing by forgiving others.

Begin the process of forgiveness today. Take time to pray, asking God for His power of forgiveness and for true freedom and healing from the harm done to you.

Reflective Reading: Psalm 147:3; Isaiah 43:1, 61; Jeremiah 17:14, 33:6; Matthew 6:14

DAILY GRATITUDE

GOALS FOR MY
THINKING AND LIVING

Overcoming Negative Habits

WEEK 6

"DO NOT BE OVERCOME BY EVIL, BUT OVERCOME EVIL WITH GOOD."

———

Romans 12:21 (NIV)

"YOU, DEAR CHILDREN, ARE FROM GOD AND HAVE OVERCOME THEM, BECAUSE THE ONE WHO IS IN YOU IS GREATER THAN THE ONE WHO IS IN THE WORLD."

———

1 John 4:4 (NIV)

Read *Telling Yourself the Truth*, chapters 11 and 12

The Power of the Amazing Brain

GENESIS 1:27 (NLT)

"God created human beings in His own image. In the image of God he created them; male and female he created them."

PSALMS 139:13–15 (NLT)

"You made all the delicate, inner parts of my body and knit me together in my mother's womb. Thank you for making me so wonderfully complex! Your workmanship is marvelous—how well I know it. You watched me as I was being formed in utter seclusion, as I was woven together in the dark of the womb."

Humans were created by God in His image. As He is a Creator, He made us with the capabilities to do the same in our sphere. We use and develop these abilities through the power of our brains. The human brain is the most complex organ in our world, controlling everything mental, spiritual, and physical in our being. It has us think, learn, make decisions, create, and have emotions while at the same time breathe, blink, and beat our hearts. A piece of brain tissue the size of a grain of sand contains 100,000 neurons and 1 billion synapses (places where neurons connect), allowing the formation of 100 trillion to 1,000 trillion connections, which is at least 1,000 times the number of stars in our galaxy. The exponential power of neuron connections creates a virtually unlimited storage capacity.

Our brains have the ability to adapt, grow, and expand throughout our lives through the process of neuroplasticity.[27] Neuroplasticity allows the brain to improve and heal from injury by physically and functionally reorganizing itself. We can think of neuroplasticity in the brain like a muscle: in the same way a muscle enhances by consistent exercise or atrophies by lack thereof, our brains can be strengthened or weakened by our environment, habits, thinking, and emotions. Strengthening positive habits and thoughts, such as rest, exercise, hydration, nutrition, orderliness, work, deep and abstract thinking, temperance, etc., will enhance neuroplasticity. As we improve ourselves, neuroplasticity will improve our brains and health, expanding our mental capacity, developing new thinking patterns, and obtaining greater wisdom than we thought we could reach. All of this leads to discovery of deeper meaning in life and greater life satisfaction. God has designed us with incredible brains! It is through the power of our brains that we can be delivered from depression and anxiety.

What does it mean to be made in the image of God? Reflect on God's goodness in creating your brain with neuroplasticity. Pray, asking God to improve your brain and lead you to greater health.

Reflective Reading: 2 Corinthians 3:18; Colossians 3:10

DAILY GRATITUDE

1 . . . .
. . . .

2 . . . .
. . . .

3 . . . .
. . . .

4 . . . .
. . . .

5 . . . .
. . . .

MY REFLECTION

Food for Thought

2 TIMOTHY 3:16, 17 (NLT)

"All Scripture is inspired by God and is useful to teach us what is true and to make us realize what is wrong in our lives. It corrects us when we are wrong and teaches us to do what is right. God uses it to prepare and equip his people to do every good work."

PSALM 119:97–104 (NLT)

"Oh, how I love your instructions! I think about them all day long. Your commands make me wiser than my enemies, for they are my constant guide. Yes, I have more insight than my teachers, for I am always thinking of your laws. I am even wiser than my elders, for I have kept your commandments. I have refused to walk on any evil path, so that I may remain obedient to your word. I haven't turned away from your regulations, for you have taught me well. How sweet your words taste to me; they are sweeter than honey. Your commandments give me understanding; no wonder I hate every false way of life."

Abstract thinking is considering and analyzing concepts beyond what we can physically see. It stimulates the frontal lobe and neuroplasticity, increasing intellect and strengthening brain function. It promotes positive, rational patterns of thought and is often associated with intelligence.

An example of abstract thinking in practice is Solomon. After becoming king of Israel, God appeared to him, offering him whatever he wanted. Solomon requested wisdom to better lead God's people. God granted it, and he became the wisest man to ever live. At the end of his life, he wrote the book of Proverbs to encapsulate and share this wisdom. In his opening thesis, he stated, "The fear of the Lord is the beginning of wisdom" (Proverbs 1:7, NIV). The foundation of all he knew, the basis for all brain improvement, is knowing God and following His instructions. We know God and learn His instructions through His Word. Scripture is therefore the best source for prompting abstract thinking.

The principles of Scripture stir the highest order of thinking, its deep insights providing us with a lifetime of study and consideration. The more we study it, the more we will grow in wisdom and in our capacity for understanding, developing our minds and protecting them from atrophy. Its treasure trove of truth encourages useful, sound thought-processing and offers guidance for all of life's problems.

Write a principle of Scripture you want to contemplate. How can you apply it to your life? Pray, asking God to improve your mind as you daily spend time reading the Bible.

Reflective Reading: Deuteronomy 6:6, 7; Proverbs 1; Ecclesiastes 12:13; James 1:5

DAILY GRATITUDE

1 . . . .
. . . .
2 . . . .
. . . .
3 . . . .
. . . .
4 . . . .
. . . .
5 . . . .
. . . .

MY REFLECTION

Dealing With Addiction

1 CORINTHIANS 6:2 (NLT)

"You say, 'I am allowed to do anything'—but not everything is good for you. And even though 'I am allowed to do anything,' I must not become a slave to anything."

2 PETER 2:19 (NLT)

"They promise freedom, but they themselves are slaves of sin and corruption. For you are a slave to whatever controls you."

ROMANS 6:18, 19 (NLT)

"Now you are free from your slavery to sin, and you have become slaves to righteous living. Because of the weakness of your human nature, I am using the illustration of slavery to help you understand all this. Previously, you let yourselves be slaves to impurity and lawlessness, which led ever deeper into sin. Now you must give yourselves to be slaves to righteous living so that you will become holy."

Addictions are habits that cause us to feel an overwhelming compulsion to continue them. We become dependent upon them, making us desire them more and giving us withdrawals when stopping them. Addictions of every form suppress our frontal lobes, inhibiting the brain's ability to function. Unfortunately, society has come to adopt addiction as commonplace and sometimes even necessary for daily living. Routines are often developed around satisfying addictions and cravings throughout the day. It's not uncommon to hear people say they "cannot function" without this or that substance or action. We all too frequently do not recognize that the things we think are helping us are actually enslaving us, keeping us from optimal health.

When Paul wrote to the Romans, he asked them to evaluate the actions of slavery to sin versus "slavery" to righteousness. If we are slaves to sin, we cannot get out of it, but if we become "slaves" to righteousness, we gain power to choose better things for ourselves, freedom to not be subject to sin, and hope of holiness. In righteousness we have true liberty. It is not God's will for us to be enslaved to detrimental habits. God desires our freedom and through Christ made it a fact: "in all these things we are more than conquerors through him who loved us" (Romans 8:37, NIV). In Jesus, we have victory over our sins and addictions. No matter how impossible overcoming may seem, we can believe the truth: since Christ has overcome, we have His power to overcome.

What addictions are you struggling with in life? How would being a "slave to righteousness" help you? Pray, claiming the freedom promised you over addiction through Jesus.

Reflective Reading: Romans 8:31; 1 Corinthians 15:57

DAILY GRATITUDE

1 ....

2 ....

3 ....

4 ....

5 ....

MY REFLECTION

The Dangers of Alcohol

PROVERBS 20:1 (NLT)

"Wine produces mockers; alcohol leads to brawls. Those led astray by drink cannot be wise."

1 THESSALONIANS 5:6–8 (NIV)

"So, then, let us not be like others, who are asleep, but let us be awake and sober. For those who sleep, sleep at night, and those who get drunk, get drunk at night. But since we belong to the day, let us be sober, putting on faith and love as a breastplate, and the hope of salvation as a helmet."

EPHESIANS 5:18 (NLT)

"Don't be drunk with wine, because that will ruin your life. Instead, be filled with the Holy Spirit."

Alcohol is a widely accepted mind-altering substance. Many people will drink socially as part of a gathering or party. Others consume it as a coping mechanism for stress or pain. Alcohol is often praised for the "happy feelings" which come from being tipsy or for its ability to numb the mind. However, its effects are dangerous. Alcohol contributes to cancer, liver disease, heart disease, high blood pressure, and stroke, among other diseases. By nature, it is addictive. It suppresses frontal lobe function and rational thinking, hindering us from making wise choices. It causes learning difficulties and contributes to dementia. It also prohibits our ability for self-restraint, which is why many have unwittingly performed outbursts of evil action under its influence, causing physical and emotional injury to strangers and loved ones alike.[28]

Throughout Scripture, alcohol is consistently used to illustrate sin. Drunkenness is listed among other sins as an action barring us from eternal life, being considered a sin for both the actions done while drunk and the altered, debased state of mind it creates. Soberness, on the other hand, is equated with rationality, watchfulness, prayer, earnestness, and vigilance. We are called to always be sober-minded to avoid temptation, spend time with Jesus, think aright, and share the gospel with others.

God created us to have clear minds. He desires us to avoid anything that weakens our health and thinking. He wants us to have the power of self-restraint so that we can be in full control of ourselves and our minds. As an alternative to substances, He offers us His Spirit and peace. He can help us cope with the struggles of life in healthy ways. We have an abundant life waiting for us in Jesus free of the things which harm us.

How can you be sober-minded? Pray, asking God to help you overcome substances affecting your mind.

Reflective Reading: 1 Corinthians 5:11; Galatians 5:21; 1 Peter 4:7, 5:8

DAILY GRATITUDE

1 . . . .
. . . .

2 . . . .
. . . .

3 . . . .
. . . .

4 . . . .
. . . .

5 . . . .
. . . .

MY REFLECTION

The Pitfalls of Indulgence

DANIEL 5:1, 2 (NLT)

"Belshazzar the king made a great feast for 1,000 of his lords, and drank wine with them. While Belshazzar was drinking the wine, he gave orders to bring in the gold and silver cups that his predecessor, Nebuchadnezzar, had taken from the Temple in Jerusalem. He wanted to drink from them with his nobles, his wives, and his concubines."

Babylon was under siege by the Medo-Persian army. Rather than diligently keeping his eye on the grave situation of his city, in a false sense of security the young king, Belshazzar, threw a party. As feasting progressed, with reason decreased by intoxication, he commanded for the gold and silver vessels taken from the temple in Jerusalem to be brought out to drink from and defame. He proceeded to openly mock God by worshiping his false gods with the sacred vessels.

Suddenly, a mysterious hand appeared, writing on the wall. Belshazzar was terrified—his face turned pale, his knees knocked together, and his legs failed him. He immediately called for the "wise men" of Babylon, but they were unable to interpret the handwriting. At the suggestion of the queen, the prophet Daniel was called to decipher the message. Daniel affirmed it was God whose hand had written the words. In the writing, divine judgment was pronounced: Belshazzar was

"weighed on the balances and [had] not measured up" (Daniel 5:27, NLT). Belshazzar was killed that night and Babylon was taken over by the Medo-Persian Empire.

Belshazzar's actions displayed his arrogance and self-indulgence. He presumed military superiority rather than leading the defense of his city. Instead of accomplishing the tasks before him, he sought a life of ease and self-gratification. Absorbed in evil pleasure and intoxication, Belshazzar chose to defy God. He paraded himself as one higher than God in drinking from the cups of the temple. In disgracing the holy, he demonstrated where his heart was. He hadn't measured up to God's standard, so he was left to the consequences of his choices. God had given Belshazzar time and opportunity to repent, to turn to God from his wicked deeds, but he refused, deciding to continue in pride.

Arrogance and indulgence lead us to choices against God. God is merciful. He gives us time to turn to Him, but we have to choose to turn. He will not force us. Jesus is offering freedom and salvation without condemnation to all who choose it.

What keeps you from turning to Jesus today? What does it mean to have salvation in Christ? Pray, asking God to free you from arrogance and self-indulgence.

Reflective Reading: Proverbs 11:2, 16:18; Ezekiel 18:30–32; Ephesians 2:1–10

DAILY GRATITUDE

1 . . . .
. . . .

2 . . . .
. . . .

3 . . . .
. . . .

4 . . . .
. . . .

5 . . . .
. . . .

MY REFLECTION

Resisting Temptation

1 CORINTHIANS 10:13 (NLT)

"The temptations in your life are no different from what others experience. And God is faithful. He will not allow the temptation to be more than you can stand. When you are tempted, he will show you a way out so that you can endure."

HEBREWS 2:18 (NLT)

"Since He Himself has gone through suffering and testing, He is able to help us when we are being tested."

We are often rightly told we must resist temptation, but how do we actually do that? Much of what surrounds us—many movies, pornography, and some even advertisements—allure us to immorality.

Joseph had many temptations. As a young man, he was a slave of Potiphar in Egypt, Pharaoh's captain of the guard. His faithfulness, hard-working character, and devotion to God made him quite prosperous. Potiphar was pleased with Joseph's success, recognizing that God was with him. He promoted Joseph to be the overseer of his entire household, trusting him so much that he did not even know what he owned. Potiphar's wife also noticed Joseph's accomplishments. She became interested in the good-looking young man and began to present numerous sexual temptations to him. Joseph was so deeply trusted that no one would have known if he had chosen to fornicate with his master's wife, and she knew it. He responded to her advances, "How could I do such a wicked thing? It would be a great sin against God" (Genesis 39:9, NLT). His focus was his faithfulness to God, and he wanted nothing to stand in the way. When confronted by her with a direct sexual pass, Joseph ran away, fleeing the temptation.

When Jesus was on the earth, He was tempted as we are. Whenever given a proposition from the Devil, He responded with "It is written," quoting Scripture and expounding upon it (Matthew 4:4, NIV). With God's Word, each temptation was successfully resisted.

We must choose to fully follow God. Our relationship with and determination to be faithful to Him provide us strength to withstand temptations. Knowing God's Word gives us the key to overcome each one. When tempted, notice what prompted it, pray to conquer it, and quote Scripture to combat it. As someone who has successfully thwarted every temptation, Jesus is ever willing and able to help us resist ours.

What temptations do you struggle with? Write a Bible verse to claim when you face them. Pray, asking God for His strength and Word to overcome temptation.

Reflective Reading: Matthew 4:1–11, 26:41; Luke 22:40; 2 Timothy 2:22; Hebrews 4:15

DAILY GRATITUDE

1 . . . .
. . . .
2 . . . .
. . . .
3 . . . .
. . . .
4 . . . .
. . . .
5 . . . .
. . . .

MY REFLECTION

Reflection and Control

1 PETER 5:8 (NLT)

"Stay alert! Watch out for your great enemy, the devil. He prowls around like a roaring lion, looking for someone to devour."

GENESIS 4:7 (NLT)

"You will be accepted if you do what is right… Sin is crouching at the door, eager to control you. But you must subdue it and be its master."

PSALM 91:3 (NLT)

"For he will rescue you from every trap and protect you from deadly disease."

With the hustle and bustle of life and the constant "go! go! go!" messaging we receive from our culture, taking time away to focus our minds through reflection is critical to maintaining our health, yet increasingly difficult. In today's world more so than at any other time in history, we are the daily target in a war for our minds. We are bombarded with an abundance of addictive media everywhere we go. Companies spend billions of dollars trying to capture and hold our attention however they can. In grabbing our brains' attention, they hope to influence our thoughts and emotions. More concerning is the fact that we are also in a spiritual war for the allegiance of our minds. The devil is trying to captivate and distract us from Jesus as a means of ensuring our demise, using whatever means necessary. While there are benefits of living in a technology age, these two wars can unfortunately work together for each other's advantage. Knowing that the powers of both the physical and spiritual world are constantly vying for our attention and allegiance proves we must be on our guard to ensure we do not fall prey to their efforts, being vigilant toward the things to which we choose to devote our mind's attention.

A practical way we can daily take more time to reflect on life and control what we see is to set boundaries with media and devices. Having a digital sabbath with intentional time in nature, with family, or in other healthy activities allows us to keep control of our minds by resting our brains and giving us time to think. Thankfully, we are not striving in the war for our minds alone. God can free us from the traps set by those who would celebrate our downfall. When we commit our minds to Him, He will enable and ennoble us to resist those things which so easily divert us away from God.

How do you plan to take time to reflect? Pray, submitting your mind to God and asking Him to strengthen you against all things that would lead you away from Him.

Reflective Reading: Psalm 18:6; James 4:7, 8

DAILY GRATITUDE

1 . . . .

2 . . . .

3 . . . .

4 . . . .

5 . . . .

MY REFLECTION

Principles for Overcoming Addictions

Like many of us, King Solomon struggled with addiction. In his later years, after breaking free from his addictions, he wrote the books of Ecclesiastes and Proverbs. Speaking from personal experience, he told of how he fell into addiction: "I said to myself, 'Come on, let's try pleasure. Let's look for the "good things" in life.' After much thought, I decided to cheer myself with wine... I hired wonderful singers, both men and women, and had many beautiful concubines. I had everything a man could desire... Anything I wanted, I would take. I denied myself no pleasure... So I came to hate life" (Ecclesiastes 2:1–17, NLT). What he thought would bring happiness ended up bringing him disdain for life itself. He learned that true joy is found in following God's ideals. He expounds on the wisdom of God's instructions, admonishing all to follow them to avoid the addictions he fell into: "My child, pay attention to what I say. Listen carefully to my words. Don't lose sight of them. Let them penetrate deep into your heart, for they bring life to those who find them, and healing to their whole body" (Proverbs 4:20–22, NLT).

The things we are addicted to are frequently things we don't need or aren't good for us. Think about it: could it ever satisfy us if it was never truly what we needed or wanted for our future?

How do we break free? Here are five principles for overcoming addictions:

- **Acknowledge that the habit is destructive.** Addictions have adverse health and relational consequences.

- **Choose to overcome the addiction.** The power of the will is much stronger than we think. (Philippians 4:13).

- **Claim God's promises on your behalf.** God's promises are still for us today. He promises us victory over all sin and things which control us: "But thank God! He gives us victory over sin and death through our Lord Jesus Christ" (1 Corinthians 15:57, NLT).

- **Rely on spiritual resources and other supportive programs.** Pray, study Scripture, seek spiritual and professional counsel, and spend time with godly friends and family. Join a 12-step program for your addiction. (Psalm 34:17).

- **Let God work.** Ask God to give you the victory He promises from your addictions. He will accomplish it. (Zechariah 4:6).

Breaking free from addictions is possible by God's grace. Sometimes we are miraculously delivered from our addictions instantly. Other times we have to put in much effort, hard work, and prayer to gain freedom. Whatever your journey is, remember that Jesus is by your side. Unite with Him and work with Him. In Christ, there is no such thing as failure, impossibility, or defeat.

Are there addictions in your life you're struggling with? What are steps to take to overcome them? Write them out. Pray, claiming God's victory over your addictions.

DAILY GRATITUDE

GOALS FOR MY THINKING AND LIVING

Dealing With Loss

WEEK 7

IT'S IN THE VALLEYS I GROW

"SOMETIMES LIFE SEEMS HARD TO BEAR,
FULL OF SORROW, TROUBLE, AND WOE,
IT'S THEN I HAVE TO REMEMBER,
THAT IT'S IN THE VALLEYS I GROW.

I DO NOT ALWAYS UNDERSTAND,
WHY THINGS HAPPEN AS THEY DO,
BUT I AM VERY SURE OF ONE THING,
MY LORD WILL SEE ME THROUGH.

FORGIVE ME LORD, FOR COMPLAINING,
WHEN I'M FEELING VERY LOW,
JUST GIVE ME A GENTLE REMINDER,
THAT IT'S IN THE VALLEY I GROW.

CONTINUE TO STRENGTHEN ME LORD,
AND USE MY LIFE EACH DAY,
TO SHARE YOUR LOVE WITH OTHERS,
AND HELP THEM FIND THEIR WAY.

THANK YOU FOR THE VALLEYS LORD,
FOR THIS ONE THING I KNOW,
THE MOUNTAIN TOPS ARE GLORIOUS,
BUT IT'S IN THE VALLEYS I GROW!"

Jane Eggleston

Read *Telling Yourself the Truth,* **chapters 13 and 14**

Grief in Loss

PSALM 34:18 (NLT)

"The Lord is close to the brokenhearted; he rescues those whose spirits are crushed."

PSALMS 31:9 (NLT)

"Have mercy on me, Lord, for I am in distress. Tears blur my eyes. My body and soul are withering away."

Experiencing loss of any form can be so heavy that it causes even the strongest of people to crumble under the weight of grief. Enduring after the loss of a loved one, career, material good, bodily function, or personal integrity can often seem impossible. Because we live in a sinful world, we all will deal with loss—it's an unfortunate, unavoidable reality. Grief is important, being the natural, healthy response to loss. It heals us from our loss and should never be condemned. If we withhold emotion or do not complete the grieving process, we can suffer severe negative health outcomes and never fully heal.

There are many examples throughout Scripture of people experiencing grief. The book of Lamentations was written by Jeremiah detailing his grief over the exile of Jerusalem. The Psalms are filled with vivid illustrations of David's grief as he encountered seemingly endless difficulties in his life. Jesus, upon seeing the tomb of Lazarus, wept over the loss of His friend, even though He knew that He was about to raise him from the dead. In the final hours of Christ's life, He was so overcome by grief He thought He might die.

Each person works through grief in their own way. Jeremiah used gratitude in his grief: "The faithful love of the Lord never ends! His mercies never cease. Great is his faithfulness; his mercies begin afresh each morning" (Lamentations 3:22, 23, NLT). David clung to his faith in God: "But I trust in your unfailing love. I will rejoice because you have rescued me. I will sing to the Lord because he is good to me" (Psalm 13:5, 6, NLT). Jesus prayed (John 17).

However we handle our grief, God is our biggest aid. He knows our sorrows and promises to send us the Comforter, the Holy Spirit. He does not cause our pain. We will never be the same after loss, and that's OK. God can use it to help us grow in faith and be better, stronger people. Through Him, we can heal and live an abundant life again.

Are you grieving something right now? How do you normally handle grief? How can God help you grieve? Pray, asking God for the Comforter and healing.

Reflective Reading: Psalm 17, 34:18, 62; Lamentations 2:11, 18; Matthew 26:38; John 11:33–36

DAILY GRATITUDE

1 . . . .

. . . .

2 . . . .

. . . .

3 . . . .

. . . .

4 . . . .

. . . .

5 . . . .

. . . .

MY REFLECTION

Guilt in Grief

PROVERBS 14:13 (NLT)

"Laughter can conceal a heavy heart, but when the laughter ends, the grief remains."

PSALM 94:19 (NIV)

"When anxiety was great within me, your consolation brought me joy."

1 PETER 5:7 (NLT)

"Give all your worries and cares to God, for he cares about you."

1 JOHN 1:9 (NLT)

"If we confess our sins to him, he is faithful and just to forgive us our sins and to cleanse us from all wickedness."

In grieving a loss, many of us experience guilt. We may feel remorse for something we did or said, or regret not saying or doing something, rehearsing the thoughts in our minds. Perhaps we feel responsibility for the loss by an action or inaction, blaming ourselves, thinking, "if I had only…" or "it's all my fault." As humans, we make mistakes, even when well-intended, so sometimes we have reason to feel guilty. However, these thoughts and feelings are most often irrational and the result of cognitive distortions we develop in our attempt to make sense of the loss. In seeking a rationale, we blame ourselves to give us a false sense of control in the situation when we never actually had any. These feelings can make it difficult to move forward in life after experiencing a loss. Even when we try to move on, as new routines and new relationships begin, we can develop feelings of guilt for doing so.

God never designed for us to continue living in guilt. He desires us to come to Him, replacing our anxiety and guilt with joy and freedom. It is OK to have new experiences and positive feelings while we are still grieving; in fact, it is a part of healing. There is hope in Christ, and reason to keep living after loss. When feeling guilty, we can reflect: did I have any control in this situation? Was it ever in my control? What knowledge did I have then? What were my intentions? If we made a mistake, we should seek forgiveness from others, God, and ourselves. If we've misplaced guilt, feeling we've done something wrong when we haven't, then we can acknowledge the feelings to let them go. God is ready to forgive us of any wrongdoings or take away guilt which never belonged to us.

How have you experienced guilt from loss? Is it something you need forgiveness for, or a distortion? How can you reframe your distortions with the truth God says about you and your loss? Pray, asking God to take your feelings of guilt and help you move on from the loss.

Reflective Reading: John 3:17; Romans 8:1

DAILY GRATITUDE

1 . . . .

. . . .

2 . . . .

. . . .

3 . . . .

. . . .

4 . . . .

. . . .

5 . . . .

. . . .

MY REFLECTION

Anger in Grief

EPHESIANS 4:26, 27 (NLT)

"'And don't sin by letting anger control you.' Don't let the sun go down while you are still angry, for anger gives a foothold to the devil."

Anger is a common component of dealing with loss. The anger we experience when grieving can be toward God, others, no one in particular, or ourselves. If we internalize our anger, we become calloused, resentful, and bitter, never fully working through our pain, completing the grieving process, or healing. Therefore, it is critical for us to acknowledge and express our anger in a healthy way rather than letting it fester.

During a severe drought, Elijah was directed by God to go live with a non-Israelite woman and her son. After a time, her son became sick and died. In her grief, she exclaimed: "O man of God, what have you done to me? Have you come here to point out my sins and kill my son?" (1 Kings 17:17, 18, NLT). Out of anger she lashed out at Elijah and, by extension, God, blaming them for her son's death. God revealed His care and power by raising her son from the dead. Job was angry with God after the deaths of all his children, the loss of all his possessions, and painful sores came upon his body. He blamed God for his suffering: "But it is God who has wronged me" (Job 19:6, NLT). He complained that God seemed in control only to continue his suffering. Job went to God, talking to Him about his anger. God corrected Job's misplacement of blame and helped him heal from his loss.

God cares when we are dealing with loss. He isn't the one to blame, Satan is. He never said we couldn't be angry when something is unjust, He said He doesn't want anger to linger or control us. Unresolved anger gives the devil a foothold in our lives. It doesn't help our problems or our grief, but only leads us to harm. The best way to work through anger is to confide honestly in God. He understands anger is a part of grief. He is not afraid of our questions and is merciful to our misunderstandings. He will help us process our anger, rightly place our blame, and heal. If we let Him, He will replace our anger with peace.

What was a time you have been angry from loss? How does going to God help you work through your anger? Pray, asking God for understanding in your anger and healing from your loss.

Reflective Reading: Psalm 37:7–9, 77, 147:3

DAILY GRATITUDE

1 . . . .

. . . .

2 . . . .

. . . .

3 . . . .

. . . .

4 . . . .

. . . .

5 . . . .

. . . .

MY REFLECTION

Depression in Grief

JOB 7:11–16 (NLT)

"I cannot keep from speaking. I must express my anguish. My bitter soul must complain… I think, 'My bed will comfort me, and sleep will ease my misery,' but then you shatter me with dreams and terrify me with visions… I hate my life and don't want to go on living."

PSALM 13 (NLT)

"O Lord, how long will you forget me? Forever? How long will you look the other way? How long must I struggle with anguish in my soul, with sorrow in my heart every day?… But I trust in your unfailing love. I will rejoice because you have rescued me. I will sing to the Lord because he is good to me."

As the realization of the extent of permanent loss sinks in, the ensuing pain often causes us to experience depression. Depression stems from feelings of extreme sadness and hopelessness. These feelings are natural to loss, but can also be caused by cognitive distortions preying on our minds in our heightened emotional stress. If not dealt with, depression leads us to prolonged, prodigious despair.

Job experienced major depression following his great loss. He couldn't escape his despair, even when sleeping. His depression was so severe that he would have rather died than continue suffering. He couldn't feel God's presence to help. David in Psalms shared his experience of depression and feeling forgotten by God. He went to God in his hurting, pouring out his feelings and asking God to answer him. Amidst his feelings, he proclaimed hope in God, which gave him strength to endure his depression.

Trusting in God doesn't mean we won't feel depressed during grief, it means He gives us hope to cling to. We may feel forgotten by God. We may not be able to sense His presence near us. However, we do not have to rely on our feelings. God promised He hasn't forgotten us. He is ever near and working to our aid. We can productively process depression by acknowledging how much the loss has affected our lives, reflecting with gratitude on the many positive experiences we had before and after the loss, and seeking what we can learn from the loss. Allowing ourselves to experience and express our feelings helps us move toward resolution instead of becoming trapped by depression.

How can depression be a reflection of the positive things you miss from the loss? How can gratitude for those things honor what was lost, allowing you to move toward resolution? Pray, claiming God's promises over your feelings and asking God to help you work through them.

Reflective Reading: Psalm 73:26; Isaiah 44:21, 49:14–16

DAILY GRATITUDE

1 . . . .
. . . .

2 . . . .
. . . .

3 . . . .
. . . .

4 . . . .
. . . .

5 . . . .
. . . .

MY REFLECTION

Acceptance in Grief

JOB 1:21 (NLT)

"I came naked from my mother's womb, and I will be naked when I leave. The Lord gave me what I had, and the Lord has taken it away. Praise the name of the Lord!"

Acceptance in grief fully acknowledges our new reality and seeks to live in it rather than resist it. It recognizes the full extent of the loss, taking the opportunity to honor the loss and move forward from it with new routines and new, fuller perspectives of it and ourselves. We accept any real responsibility we had in our loss and let go of our distortions and what we could not control. We are better able to regulate our emotions and take care of ourselves, as well as experience positive, hopeful feelings about life and the future. Accepting our loss does not mean we forget or minimize the significance of it or miss it any less. It means we have allowed ourselves to learn from and grow through it instead of becoming closed and stunted by it.

Jacob, after working 14 years to marry his beloved Rachel, lost her from childbirth with their second son, Benjamin: "After a very hard delivery, the midwife finally exclaimed, 'Don't be afraid—you have another son!' Rachel was about to die, but with her last breath she named the baby Ben-oni (which means 'son of my sorrow'). The baby's father, however, called him Benjamin (which means 'son of my right hand')" (Genesis 35:17, 18, NLT). Jacob was in great sorrow over the loss of Rachel. He buried her where she died and erected a pillar in memoriam to her. In renaming their son, Jacob recognized the love he had for Rachel and the strength she had provided him in life—as that of a "right hand." He focused on the positive memories of their relationship, was grateful for the two children they had, and did what he could to honor her legacy.

God never desired for us to experience loss, but He is caring, giving us the strength to endure our pain while providing opportunity for reflection and renewal when we do experience it. He desires us to reach a place of acceptance. We can grow to become stronger, more grateful people, better equipped to love, serve, and empathize compassionately with the world around us.

How can you develop the spirit of acceptance in grief? Pray, asking God for strength to accept your loss, grow from it, and move forward with a renewed perspective to serve Him and others.

Reflective Reading: Genesis 35:16–20, 48:7; Matthew 5:4; John 14:1; 2 Corinthians 1:3, 4

DAILY GRATITUDE

1 . . . .

. . . .

2 . . . .

. . . .

3 . . . .

. . . .

4 . . . .

. . . .

5 . . . .

. . . .

MY REFLECTION

Jesus Understands

JOHN 3:16 (NLT)

"For this is how God loved the world: He gave his one and only Son, so that everyone who believes in him will not perish but have eternal life."

ISAIAH 53:3, 6 (NLT)

"He was despised and rejected—a man of sorrows, and acquainted with deepest grief… But he was pierced for our rebellion, crushed for our sins. He was beaten so we could be whole. He was whipped so we could be healed."

HEBREWS 4:15 (NLT)

"This High Priest of ours understands our weaknesses, for he faced all the same testings we do, yet he did not sin."

"The spotless Son of God hung upon the cross, His flesh lacerated with stripes; those hands so often reached out in blessing, nailed to the wooden bars; those feet so tireless on ministries of love, spiked to the tree; that royal head pierced by the crown of thorns; those quivering lips shaped to the cry of woe. And all that he endured—the blood drops that flowed from His head, His hands, His feet, the agony that racked His frame, and the unutterable anguish that filled His soul at the hiding of His Father's face— speaks to each child of humanity, declaring, it is for thee that the Son of God consents... and this from love to thee" (*The Desire of Ages*, p. 755).

Christ is acquainted with grief and loss. He witnessed it in all its ugly forms as He walked about the earth. He experienced the death of loved ones and the betrayal of friends. In partaking of the life of man, His heart was stirred to compassion, His body moved to tears. Finally, He experienced the loss of complete separation from His Father for the first time in all eternity and that of His own life in suffering a cruel death.

By becoming a man, Christ experienced the pain of loss as we do. In every area of life, He was tempted and struggled. He can relate to every human woe, to each ounce of pain, and can identify with our suffering. Out of love for us and joy at the thought of our salvation, He endured our lot to empathize with and save us. Whatever you are suffering right now, Jesus can relate to you, He can heal you, and He can save you. His tender, compassionate heart is still ever awakened to sympathy by our suffering, weeping with those who weep. At the point of greatest discouragement, hardest trial, and utmost loss, divine help and comfort is nearest.

How does Jesus relate to your loss? Pray, asking God to help you recognize His sympathy and thanking God for His love for you.

Reflective Reading: Isaiah 53; Hebrews 12:2

DAILY GRATITUDE

1 ....
  ....
2 ....
  ....
3 ....
  ....
4 ....
  ....
5 ....
  ....

MY REFLECTION

....
....
....
....
....
....
....
....
....
....

Hope in Loss

ISAIAH 25:8 (NLT)

"He will swallow up death forever! The Sovereign Lord will wipe away all tears. He will remove forever all insults and mockery against His land and people. The Lord has spoken!"

JOB 19:25, 26 (NIV)

"But as for me, I know that my Redeemer lives, and he will stand upon the earth at last. And after my body has decayed, yet in my body I will see God!"

ROMANS 8:23 (NLT)

"We long for our bodies to be released from sin and suffering. We, too, wait with eager hope for the day when God will give us our full rights as his adopted children."

When we experience loss of any kind, we should hold on to hope. Mourning and sorrow are an undesired reality of life on earth, but we can be encouraged that, though our lives will be different and we cannot change the past, our loss will not always be permanent. The Bible assures us that Christ has overcome death. We have the promise of the resurrection for ourselves and those we have lost, which will make us free from death and its effects. More than this, we have the promise of an earth made new where grief and loss will be no more. We will have perfect reconciliation with God and each other:

"Then I saw a new heaven and a new earth, for the old heaven and the old earth had disappeared. And the sea was also gone. And I saw the holy city, the new Jerusalem, coming down from God out of heaven like a bride beautifully dressed for her husband. I heard a loud shout from the throne, saying, 'Look, God's home is now among his people! He will live with them, and they will be his people. God himself will be with them. He will wipe every tear from their eyes, and there will be no more death or sorrow or crying or pain. All these things are gone forever'" (Revelation 21:1–4, NLT).

While it may seem we have no solace, as we reflect on and internalize the promises of Scripture in faith, our spirit of grief will find solace in hope. Jesus made this hope reality. As you experience your loss, look beyond the portals of death and sorrow. Look to hope! God has saved you. He has a future, a plan, and a hope for you. You are his child, and He cares for you deeply.

How can you claim hope in your grief? Pray, asking God for hope and faith in His promises.

> **Reflective Reading: Psalm 30:5, 42:11; Isaiah 51:11; 1 Corinthians 15:51–55; 1 Thessalonians 4:13–18**

DAILY GRATITUDE

1 . . . .
. . . .

2 . . . .
. . . .

3 . . . .
. . . .

4 . . . .
. . . .

5 . . . .
. . . .

MY REFLECTION

Principles for Learning to Trust: Take Your Questions to God

The book of Habakkuk is a conversation between Habakkuk and God. The dialogue is short, beginning with Habakkuk lamenting the problem of evil in the world, particularly in God's own people, Judah. God responds, revealing the impending destruction of Judah by another nation. Habakkuk questions God's righteousness in allowing them to overtake Judah, who is "more righteous than they" (Habakkuk 1:13, NLT). He awaits the Lord's reply, choosing to speak no further until he is "corrected" by God (v. 2:1). The Lord answers Habakkuk with a powerful statement: "But the just shall live by his faith" (v. 4); He then reveals the end of the wicked and the justice of God. The conversation, and the book, ends with Habakkuk's prayer, prophesying of the coming Messiah and God's ultimate salvation. He concludes with words of faith:

"Even though the fig trees have no blossoms, and there are no grapes on the vines; even though the olive crop fails, and the fields lie empty and barren; even though the flocks die in the fields, and the cattle barns are empty, yet I will rejoice in the Lord! I will be joyful in the God of my salvation! The Sovereign Lord is my strength! He makes me as surefooted as a deer, able to tread upon the heights" (Habakkuk 3:17–19, NLT).

Through communion with God, Habakkuk realized God's perspective. Despite the suffering and injustice he witnessed, he rejoiced, trusting that God would make all things right. In spite of what he could see, he had faith in the promise of God's salvation.

Habakkuk had to work through his questions to trust God. He gives us an example of how we can take our questions to God:

- Be willing to listen to God

- Be willing to be corrected

- Be willing to take God at His word and see what happens

Like Habakkuk, we may find it difficult to trust God. God isn't afraid of our questions, but invites us to "come" and "reason together" (Isaiah 1:18, NLT). The same God who spoke to Habakkuk is willing to speak to us. We may not hear an audible voice, but He will commune with us through His Word and the Holy Spirit. His promises are still valid. We may not receive the answer we are looking for, but He will give us the answer we need.

Write the questions you have for God and anything keeping you from trusting Him. Take the time you need to have a conversation with God about each one. Pray, asking God to reveal to you His trustworthiness and help you trust Him.

DAILY GRATITUDE

GOALS FOR MY
THINKING AND LIVING

Making and Staying With Positive Lifestyle Choices

WEEK 8

HE HELD MY HAND

HE HELD MY HAND IN WEAKNESS
AND HELPED ME TO BE STRONG,
HE HELD IT THROUGH THE DESERT'S HEAT
AND GAVE MY HEART A SONG.

HE HELD MY HAND IN CROOKED WAYS
AND THROUGH THE MOUNTAINS STEEP,
HE HELD IT LIKE A SHEPHERD
CARING FOR HIS SHEEP.

HE HELD MY HAND IN SORROW,
FAR MORE THAN I COULD BEAR,
I FELT HIS TENDER TOUCH
AND KNEW THAT HE WAS THERE.

HE HELD MY HAND IN DARKNESS,
IN THE BLACKNESS OF THE NIGHT,
HE HELD IT 'TILL THE MORNING
WHEN I COULD SEE THE LIGHT.

I'VE LEARNED TO HOLD HIS HAND,
I'LL CLING TO IT FOREVER,
I'LL NEVER LET IT GO,
NO, NEVER, NEVER, NEVER!

Elva E. Springer

The Motivation for Real Change

2 CORINTHIANS 5:14 (NIV)

"For Christ's love compels us."

1 JOHN 4:18 (NLT)

"Such love has no fear, because perfect love expels all fear. If we are afraid, it is for fear of punishment, and this shows that we have not fully experienced his perfect love."

1 CORINTHIANS 16:14 (NIV)

"Do everything in love."

One of the most powerful motivations for any change is fear—fear of death, sickness, loss, being looked down upon, or whatever else it may be. Fear not only affects our physical choices, but our spiritual ones. Many of us make changes because we are seeking to avoid judgment, damnation, and suffering. Unfortunately, fear often utilizes manipulation, which can be devastating when we realize it. It is difficult for any such changes to be truly heartfelt because they are all a reaction to negative stimuli, focused on what we may lose rather than what we could gain.

The only motivation more powerful than fear is love. The experience of unselfish love is the greatest agent of change. This alone is the way God seeks to transform us. Change from love is a response to good news. Love does not manipulate. It brings joy and heartfelt desire for change because it is focused on positive thinking and all we have to gain.

God loves us, and His love has the ability to transform us. When we encounter Christ on the cross and internalize for ourselves the grace He offers us, we realize He gives us the power to change for our own benefit. Christ has removed all fear, offering us complete salvation from love without condemnation. He wants us to carry the weight of fear no longer. He invites us, "Come to me, all of you who are weary and carry heavy burdens, and I will give you rest. Take my yoke upon you. Let me teach you, because I am humble and gentle at heart, and you will find rest for your souls. For my yoke is easy to bear, and the burden I give you is light" (Matthew 11:28–30, NLT). If we desire, Jesus will teach us how to live a changed life by empowering us with His Spirit and imbuing us with His love. He will take the heavy burden of fear and give us the light burden of peace and love.

Describe a moment you were motivated by fear, and then a moment you were motivated by love. What was the difference? Pray, asking God to take your burden of fear and give you motivation out of love.

Reflective Reading: John 15:13; Romans 8; 1 Corinthians 13; 1 John 4:7–19

DAILY GRATITUDE

1 . . . .
. . . .

2 . . . .
. . . .

3 . . . .
. . . .

4 . . . .
. . . .

5 . . . .
. . . .

MY REFLECTION

A New Creation: Addressing Spiritual Lifestyle

EPHESIANS 4:22-24 (NLT)

"Throw off your old sinful nature and your former way of life, which is corrupted by lust and deception. Instead, let the Spirit renew your thoughts and attitudes. Put on your new nature, created to be like God—truly righteous and holy."

2 CORINTHIANS 5:17 (NLT)

"This means that anyone who belongs to Christ has become a new person. The old life is gone; a new life has begun!"

Lifestyle deeply influences a person's experience with depression and anxiety, and our current lifestyle choices are influenced directly by our inward spiritual condition. The strength of our character determines much of our inner health when all is said and done. Developing new character strengths and virtues, such as courage, integrity, vitality, perseverance, love, kindness, temperance, forgiveness, humility, self-control, contentment, and hope, will propel us to a higher mental and physical level and to a more satisfied and fulfilled life.

Making outward changes in our lives produces a good result; however, when we allow God to transform our inner self, we become recreated from the inside out. This is God's ideal for us: "May you experience the love of Christ, though it is too great to understand fully. Then you will be made complete with all the fullness of life and power that comes from God" (Ephesians 3:19, NLT). It is through God's love that we are transformed in character to become complete, fulfilled and spiritually healthy in life.

We receive Christ's love by spending daily time with Him: "Again, the Kingdom of Heaven is like a merchant on the lookout for choice pearls. When he discovered a pearl of great value, he sold everything he owned and bought it!" (Matthew 13:45, 46, NLT). You are the pearl of great price. Christ left heaven and gave up everything to come to rescue you. He does not see you as worthless and sinful, but as what you may become through His redeeming love, so much greater beyond what you can imagine. In response to Christ's love, we see Christ as our Pearl of great price. We acquire Him by choosing to receive His love and allowing Him to change our sinful, unhealthy habits.

What character strengths do you want to possess? What spiritual habits will you implement to allow Christ to accomplish them? Pray, opening your heart to God's presence and thanking Him for making you a new creation in Jesus.

Reflective Reading: Matthew 13:44; Romans 5:1—11

DAILY GRATITUDE

1 ....

2 ....

3 ....

4 ....

5 ....

MY REFLECTION

Developing New Habits With the Spirit

GALATIANS 5:16–18 (NLT)

"So I say, let the Holy Spirit guide your lives. Then you won't be doing what your sinful nature craves. The sinful nature wants to do evil, which is just the opposite of what the Spirit wants. And the Spirit gives us desires that are the opposite of what the sinful nature desires. These two forces are constantly fighting each other, so you are not free to carry out your good intentions. But when you are directed by the Spirit, you are not under obligation to the law of Moses."

GALATIANS 2:20 (NLT)

"My old self has been crucified with Christ. It is no longer I who live, but Christ lives in me. So I live in this earthly body by trusting in the Son of God, who loved me and gave himself for me."

PSALMS 51:10–12 (NLT)

"Create in me a clean heart, O God, renew a loyal spirit within me. Do not banish me from your presence, and don't take your Holy Spirit from me. Restore to me the joy of your salvation, and make me willing to obey you."

Everyone knows their bad habits—the things we know we probably should not be doing, yet we continue to do them because they have become a part of how we cope with life. In many cases, the frequent indulgence of these bad habits can lead to, often in combination with other factors, depression and anxiety.

In adopting a new lifestyle, it can be difficult to overcome our bad habits. The good news is that Christ has promised to make us a new creation in Him and to give us a new heart (2 Corinthians 5:17, Ezekiel 36:26). He has given us the Holy Spirit, who is able to work in us and through us to conquer the habits which bring us down. While change may take time, we can rest assured knowing that the power of Christ has broken the hold of evil on us. With the Holy Spirit dwelling within us, we can choose to not be subject to our bad habits any longer and to live by faith in Him.

What bad habits do you want to overcome? What struggles do you have in working to overcome them? Take comfort in the knowledge that God is working with you. Pray, asking God for continued perseverance. Thank Him for the ways in which He has provided for you in the past. Claim the promise that He will continue to provide for your future.

Reflective Reading: Ezekiel 36:24–38; Romans 6:1–7, 8:12, 13

DAILY GRATITUDE

1 . . . .
. . . .

2 . . . .
. . . .

3 . . . .
. . . .

4 . . . .
. . . .

5 . . . .
. . . .

MY REFLECTION

Making Permanent Change

2 PETER 1:4–7 (NLT)

"And because of his glory and excellence, he has given us great and precious promises. These are the promises that enable you to share his divine nature and escape the world's corruption caused by human desires. In view of all this, make every effort to respond to God's promises. Supplement your faith with a generous provision of moral excellence, and moral excellence with knowledge, and knowledge with self-control, and self-control with patient endurance, and patient endurance with godliness, and godliness with brotherly affection, and brotherly affection with love for everyone."

Temporary changes may yield some results, but only permanent change brings lasting effects in the fight against depression and anxiety. We often don't like to make changes, especially when we don't instantly see unfavorable results in our current lifestyle. Scripture aptly illustrates our human condition: "But when grace is shown to the wicked, they do not learn righteousness" Isaiah 26:10 (NLT). The lack of immediate consequences for negative actions motivates us to continue them, and we sometimes even assume there is nothing wrong with them.

God wants us to see the long-term consequences of our choices as He does, to have a new way of thinking. He wants us to have a new character, not just new habits. Only God can produce this change in us by His grace through faith in His promises. Jesus' sacrifice on the cross demonstrates the benevolence of His character and leads us to faith that He will complete each promise He made. We can claim His promises, trusting that we have what Jesus said. Because of the power of Christ's Word, the changes we make can be permanent.

As we believe God's promises, our thinking will change. Scripture outlines the attributes we will see in our characters as we change. First is moral excellence, a code upon which we base our actions. Then is self-control—God has set us free from our old self, giving us power to make positive choices. Next, we develop patient endurance, trusting God started His work and will accomplish it in our lives. The Holy Spirit then establishes true godliness within us. Through all this, God creates brotherly affection and compassion for others in us, which is His goal, "the bond of perfection" (Colossians 3:14, NKJV). His process of change will imbue His love in our characters and give us lasting results.

What lasting changes do you need to make? Write promises from God's Word to claim to help you make those changes. Pray, asking God to help you recognize His promises and accomplish real, lasting change in you.

Reflective Reading: Isaiah 43:18, 19; 2 Corinthians 1:20; Ephesians 2:1–10

DAILY GRATITUDE

1 . . . .
. . . .

2 . . . .
. . . .

3 . . . .
. . . .

4 . . . .
. . . .

5 . . . .
. . . .

MY REFLECTION

The Power of the Will: Self-Control

PROVERBS 16:32 (NLT)

"Better to be patient than powerful; better to have self-control than to conquer a city."

PROVERBS 25:28 (NLT)

"A person without self-control is like a city with broken-down walls."

GALATIANS 5:22, 23 (NLT)

"But the Holy Spirit produces this kind of fruit in our lives: love, joy, peace, patience, kindness, goodness, faithfulness, gentleness, and self-control. There is no law against these things!"

The will is the power of human agency to choose. God has given each of us the freedom to exercise our willpower however we want, with our actions and thoughts being a result of our internal choices. If we make the right choices, we will have good outcomes and our frontal lobes will be enhanced.[29–33] Self-control is a necessary character trait in order for us to choose to do what is right. It is part of the fruit of the Holy Spirit, being available to us through Him by the application of our will to choose it. When we choose to follow God's instructions to do what is right, we co-work with Him, which allows Him to work in us and give us "the desire and the power to do what pleases him" through the Holy Spirit (Philippians 2:13, NLT). Such coworking with God amplifies our ability to exhibit self-control, thus continuing a positive cycle and producing good outcomes.

Think of coworking with God like someone driving a truck down a curvy mountain road. God provides the truck and its steering abilities, allowing the truck to move and turn. We choose where to steer. If we stop steering while driving, we could cause an accident; if we never drive the truck, we won't go anywhere. God has given us everything we need to make choices, good or bad, and then He allows us to make choices. But if we never make choices (or, drive the truck), we will never experience the good things He has promised us. God created nature and its laws. He will not always interfere with the consequences of us choosing to follow or violate them. As our physical health is dependent upon these laws, so is our mental health. He has given us the ability to choose our future. God expects us to pray and do, and He will come through for us. When we choose to co-labor with God, He gives us the self-control we need to make right choices and habits.

Reflect on the proverb: "every man is the architect of his own fortune." How will good choices influence your future? Pray, asking God for self-control to make right choices.

Reflective Reading: Jeremiah 31:33; Galatians 6:7, 8; Titus 2

DAILY GRATITUDE

1 ....
....
2 ....
....
3 ....
....
4 ....
....
5 ....
....

MY REFLECTION

Hope for the Future

HEBREWS 10:23 (NLT)

"Let us hold tightly without wavering to the hope we affirm, for God can be trusted to keep his promise."

JOB 11:18 (NLT)

"Having hope will give you courage. You will be protected and rest in safety."

ROMANS 5:5 (NLT)

"And this hope will not lead to disappointment. For we know how dearly God loves us, because he has given us the Holy Spirit to fill our hearts with his love."

When struggling with depression and anxiety, life can feel hopeless. Internalizing feelings of hopelessness compounds depression and anxiety, creating a mental block which reinforces negative thoughts and emotions, thus continuing the cycle and causing the effects to worsen. Hope, on the contrary, breaks this cycle and leads us through dire circumstances.

Studies show that hope is more important to life and survival than physical strength. An incredible story of hope is that of Ernest Shackleton and his men aboard the ship *Endurance*. In an expedition to the South Pole, the ship got stuck in the ice a day's sailing away from their supply depot. With limited supplies, they lived 10 months on the ship, then another six months on the open ice, until nearby islands came into view. The men sailed the ship's lifeboats for seven days through the frigid water until they reached an island. Then, Shackleton and select men sailed over 800 miles in brutal weather on a lifeboat to the nearest whaling station for rescue. Upon arrival, the men hiked over 30 hours to the whaling station. With help, Shackleton organized rescue operations for the rest of his men on the island, and they were all finally retrieved a few months later. Miraculously, everyone survived. Men on the ship wrote that Shackleton "never lost his optimism" as he led his men to endure the hardships. The leader of the group remaining on the island daily encouraged his men to hope, preparing for Shackleton's return on a relief ship.[34] Their hope carried them through.

Hopelessness is a death-sentence in our struggle against depression and anxiety. Hope for a better future is what sustains our striving to make positive change. We find our greatest hope looking to Jesus and the rewards promised to His redeemed: salvation and eternal life with Christ. On hard days and in every trial, cling to hope! His hope will never disappoint us.

In what areas of your life do you feel hopeless? Write a passage of Scripture to combat your feelings with the promise of hope. Pray, asking God to put His hope within you and for faith to cling to that hope in every circumstance.

Reflective Reading: Lamentations 3:24; Romans 8:18

DAILY GRATITUDE

1

2

3

4

5

MY REFLECTION

A New Purpose

2 CORINTHIANS 4:16–18 (NLT)

"That is why we never give up. Though our bodies are dying, our spirits are being renewed every day. For our present troubles are small and won't last very long. Yet they produce for us a glory that vastly outweighs them and will last forever! So we don't look at the troubles we can see now; rather, we fix our gaze on things that cannot be seen. For the things we see now will soon be gone, but the things we cannot see will last forever."

1 PETER 2:9 (NLT)

"You are royal priests, a holy nation, God's very own possession. As a result, you can show others the goodness of God, for he called you out of the darkness into his wonderful light."

Possessing a deep and abiding sense of purpose in our lives will help us sustain a strong character through even the most difficult times. In struggling with depression and anxiety, we may feel our life has no purpose or that there is no greater purpose for us to serve. Perhaps we lost sight of our purpose or became overwhelmed by heavy burdens and responsibilities in life. A sense of purpose is closely tied to finding our identity in Christ. When we enter into a saving relationship with Him, we properly identify ourselves as His children and recognize the purpose He puts on our lives. While callings vary, our purpose includes becoming an agent of change for others by sharing with them the amazing change Christ made in us. Simply, this means we reveal to others what God has revealed to us. We can accomplish our purpose by 1) embracing Christ's changes in our lives, 2) relying on Christ for continued strength, and 3) accepting God's purpose for us. Each step is one of faith by accepting the work Christ does in and through us. This process will continually provide a renewed sense of purpose, and will ultimately lead to a stronger, more virtuous character.

We began our journey with the story of God helping Elijah overcome depression and anxiety. In providing for all of his needs, God gave Elijah renewed purpose in life and work to accomplish, including passing on his mantle to train the next prophet of Israel, Elisha (1 Kings 19:15–21). Just as God gave Elijah purpose, He also desires us to have a purpose and enjoy a fulfilling life. He helps us accomplish every step needed in our recovery from depression and anxiety.

Do you feel a sense of purpose from God? If so, what is it? Pray, asking God to solidify His purpose for you and thanking Him for providing for all your needs in your journey.

> **Reflective Reading: Ecclesiastes 3:12–14; Jeremiah 29:11–13; 2 Corinthians 5:18**

DAILY GRATITUDE

1 . . . .
. . . .

2 . . . .
. . . .

3 . . . .
. . . .

4 . . . .
. . . .

5 . . . .
. . . .

MY REFLECTION

Persisting in Health

Our time together has come to a close, but your journey is just beginning as you continue to improve your health and mental capabilities. There is great work ahead of you, but also great gain. Keep persisting! You will reap the reward of your labor.

- **Persevere in your healthy habits.** Once we begin to feel better, we may be tempted to loosen up or stop our new healthy habits. We must remember that it is our healthy habits that brought us our physical and mental health. Without them, we wouldn't be where we are now. If we persist, our brains will continue to improve throughout our lives. Our full potential in optimizing our brains is ahead of us, and we only get closer to it by continuing in healthy thoughts and activities.

- **Live a balanced life.** Balance means taking time for our health. We all lead busy lives, but if we don't take time for our well-being, no one else will. We have to schedule our priorities first, making time for what is most important to our lives and health. Every few days, do a self-evaluation to check your balance.

- **Be a compassionate instructor, teaching others what you've learned.** What we have learned has helped us immensely, so why wouldn't we want to share it? As we share these principles and our own experience of them with others, it will solidify these positive lifestyle principles in ourselves. Additionally, we'll have the fulfillment of helping others and seeing them improve their lives.

Above all else, rely on Christ in all your journey. He is your Rock, your Strength, your Creator and Recreator, your Redeemer, and your Sustainer. It is through Him that you accomplish your goals. Trust Him, for He is the One who gives victory in your battles and will keep you successful throughout your life. He loves you, and His love gives you all you need.

COLOSSIANS 2:7 (NLT)

"Let your roots grow down into him, and let your lives be built on him. Then your faith will grow strong in the truth you were taught, and you will overflow with thankfulness."

EPHESIANS 3:20 (NLT)

"Now all glory to God, who is able, through his mighty power at work within us, to accomplish infinitely more than we might ask or think."

JUDE 24, 25 (NIV)

"To him who is able to keep you from stumbling and to present you before his glorious presence without fault and with great joy—to the only God our Savior be glory, majesty, power and authority, through Jesus Christ our Lord, before all ages, now and forevermore! Amen."

NUMBERS 6:24–26 (NLT)

"May the Lord bless you and protect you. May the Lord smile on you and be gracious to you. May the Lord show you his favor and give you his peace."

DAILY GRATITUDE

GOALS FOR MY
THINKING AND LIVING

References

1. Oxford University Press. (1989). Gratitude. In *Oxford English Dictionary*. (2nd ed.).

2. Emmons, R., & McCullough, M. (2003). Counting blessings versus burdens: An experimental investigation of gratitude and subjective well-being in daily life. *Journal of Personality and Social Psychology, 84*(2), 377–389.

3. Nedley, N. (1999). *Proof Positive: How to reliably combat disease and achieve optimal health through nutrition and lifestyle.* Nedley Publishing.

4. Kober, S.E., Witte, M… Wood, G. (2017). Ability to gain control over one's own brain activity and its relation to spiritual practice: A multimodal imaging study. *Frontiers in Human Neuroscience, 11*(1), 271.

5. McKinney, C. H., Antoni, M. H… McCabe, P. M. (1997). Effects of guided imagery and music (GIM) therapy on mood and cortisol in healthy adults. *Health Psychology, 16*(4), 390–400.

6. Jiang, S. Y., Ma, A., & Ramachandran, S. (2018). Negative air ions and their effects on human health and air quality improvement. *International Journal of Molecular Sciences, 19*(10), 2966.

7. Maas, J., Verheij, R. A… Groenewegen, P. P. (2009). Morbidity is related to a green living environment. *Journal of Epidemiology and Community Health, 63*(12), 967–973.

8. Nedley, N., & Ramirez, F. E. (2016). Nedley depression hit hypothesis: Identifying depression and its causes. *American Journal of Lifestyle Medicine, 10*(6), 422–428.

9. Sarris, J., Logan, A. C… International Society for Nutritional Psychiatry Research. (2015). Nutritional medicine as mainstream in psychiatry. *The Lancet Psychiatry, 2*(3), 271–274.

10. Katcher, H. I., Ferdowsian, H. R… Barnard, N. D. (2010). A worksite vegan nutrition program is well-accepted and improves health-related quality of life and work productivity. *Annals of Nutrition & Metabolism, 56*(4), 245–252.

11. Agarwal, U., Mishra, S…Barnard, N. D. (2015). A multicenter randomized controlled trial of a nutrition intervention program in a multiethnic adult population in the corporate setting reduces depression and anxiety and improves quality of life: The GEICO study. *American Journal of Health Promotion, 29*(4), 245–254.

12. Brocchi, A., Rebelos, E… Daniele, G. (2022). Effects of intermittent fasting on brain metabolism. *Nutrients, 14*(6), 1275.

13. Vaynman, S., Ying, Z… Gomez-Pinilla, F. (2006). Coupling energy metabolism with a mechanism to support brain-derived neurotrophic factor-mediated synaptic plasticity. *Neuroscience, 139*(4), 1221–1234.

14. Wu, A., Ying, Z., & Gomez-Pinilla, F. (2004). The interplay between oxidative stress and brain-derived neurotrophic factor modulates the outcome of a saturated fat diet on synaptic plasticity and cognition. *The European Journal of Neuroscience, 19*(7), 1699–1707.

15. Mattson M. P. (2008). Dietary factors, hormesis and health. *Ageing Research Reviews, 7*(1), 43–48.

16. Nedley, N. (2005). *Depression: The way out.* Nedley Publishing.

17. David, D., Cristea, I., & Hofmann, S. G. (2018). Why cognitive behavioral therapy is the current gold standard of psychotherapy. *Frontiers in Psychiatry, 9*, 4.

18. Kaczkurkin, A. N., & Foa, E. B. (2015). Cognitive-behavioral therapy for anxiety disorders: An update on the empirical evidence. *Dialogues in Clinical Neuroscience, 17*(3), 337–346.

19. Shayan, A., Taravati, M… Masoumi, S. Z. (2018). The effect of cognitive behavioral therapy on marital quality among women. *International Journal of Fertility & Sterility, 12*(2), 99–105.

20. Linardon, J., Wade, T. D… Brennan, L. (2017). The efficacy of cognitive-behavioral therapy for eating disorders: A systematic review and meta-analysis. *Journal of Consulting and Clinical Psychology, 85*(11), 1080–1094.

21. Matusiewicz, A. K., Hopwood, C. J… Lejuez, C. W. (2010). The effectiveness of cognitive behavioral therapy for personality disorders. *The Psychiatric Clinics of North America, 33*(3), 657–685.

22. Gautam, M., Tripathi, A… Gaur, M. (2020). Cognitive behavioral therapy for depression. *Indian Journal of Psychiatry, 62*(Suppl 2), S223–S229.

23. Kioulos, K. T., Alexandri, Z. H… Bergiannaki, I. D. (2017). The relationship between forgiveness, mental health and psychotherapy. *Psychiatriki, 28*(4), 349–359.

24. Weir, K. (2017). Forgiveness can improve mental and physical health. *Monitor on Psychology, 48*(1).

25. Toussaint, L. L., Williams, D. R… Everson, S. A. (2001). Forgiveness and health: Age differences in a U.S. probability sample. *Journal of Adult Development, 8*(4), 249–257.

26. vanOyen Witvliet, C., Ludwig, T. E., & Vander Laan, K. L. (2001). Granting forgiveness or harboring grudges: Implications for emotion, physiology, and health. *Psychological Science, 12*(2), 117–123.

27. Puderbaugh, M., & Emmady, P. D. (2022). *Neuroplasticity.* PubMed; StatPearls Publishing.

28. Iranpour, A., & Nakhaee, N. (2019). A review of alcohol-related harms: A recent update. *Addiction & Health, 11*(2), 129–137.

29. Baumeister, R. F. (2002). Ego depletion and self-control failure: An energy model of the self's executive function. *Self and Identity, 1*(2), 129–136.

30. Peterson, C., & Seligman, M. (2004). Self-control. In *Character strengths and virtues: A handbook and classification* (pp. 499–516). Oxford University Press.

31. Tangney, J. P., Baumeister, R. F., & Boone, A. L. (2004). High self-control predicts good adjustment, less pathology, better grades, and interpersonal success. *Journal of Personality, 72*(2), 271–324.

32. Duckworth, A. L., White, R. E… Gross, J. J. (2016). A stitch in time: Strategic self-control in high school and college students. *Journal of Educational Psychology, 108*(3), 329–341.

33. Baumeister, R., & Tierney, J. (2012). *Willpower: Rediscovering the greatest human strength.* Penguin Books.

34. Mulvaney, K. (2022, March 9). *How Ernest Shackleton's Endurance Crew Survived Almost Certain Death - HISTORY.* History.com.

Lyrics to Songs

Onward Christian Soldiers*

Onward, Christian soldiers!
Marching as to war,
Fighting false perceptions,
Feelings, pride, and more.
Christ has given battle tools:
Reason, conscience, TRUTH!
Forward into battle,
Use our WILLS to choose!

Onward, Christian soldiers!
Marching as to war,
With the cross of Jesus
Going on before.

When the Spirit of truth
is come,
To all truth He guides.
There is comfort, peace
with truth;
There is none with lies.
By deception, Satan gains
Power o'er the mind.
Through the Word of Truth, the
Spirit subdues humankind.

Onward, Christian soldiers!
Marching as to war,
With the words of Jesus
Going on before.

Minds are much like gardens;
Seeds of truth can sprout.
We must tend
them constantly;
Weeds can choke them out.
Gardening is no easy task!
We must do our part.
Christians must be vigilant—
Life's a battle march!

Onward, Christian soldiers—
Women men and youth,
Every thought we must yield
To the Spirit of truth.

I Surrender All*

All to Jesus I surrender,
Every thought I bring to You,
Casting down imaginations,
Captive only to what's true.

I surrender all!
I surrender all!
You desire Truth within me;
I surrender all.

All to Jesus I surrender
What I think will
certainly shape
Perceptions of experience,
And become a part of me.

I surrender all!
I surrender all!
You desire Truth within me;
I surrender all.

True and honest, just and pure,
And lovely things of
good report,
If there's virtue, if there's praise,
My thoughts will only be
these sort.

I surrender all!
I surrender all!
You desire Truth within me;
I surrender all.

I'm drawn by my fallen
feelings
To regret, so I must test.
Use my will, and reason,
conscience;
Am I worshiping the best?

I surrender all!
I surrender all!
What I live for is my Master,
I surrender all.

When I fear that I'm worth
nothing,
There's a Truth that sets
me free:
I am valued by the price paid,
GOD HIMSELF has died
for me!

I surrender all;
Intimate to You,
"Knowing" Truth is more
than knowledge,
I surrender all.

Feelings Come and Feelings Go**

Feelings come and feelings go,
and feelings are deceiving.

Trust alone on the word of God,
it's something worth believing.

(repeat)

*Lyrics to "Onward Christian Soldiers" and "I Surrender All" © 2005 by Anthea Hii. Anthea requests that these lyrics only be used in connection with the Nedley Depression and Anxiety Recovery Program™ in order to help others in their recovery. Used by permission.

**Sung to the tune of Yankee-Doodle.